Being Church
Where We Live

A Vision for the Body of Christ

Ron McKenzie

Kingwatch Books

Some of this material was published previously
in a booklet called the Bride of Christ (1983).

Parables — To illustrate the themes of this book, I have included
a number of parables. The people and situations described in these
parables are not real and should not be taken as such. They are all
nice people, so if one seems to be like you, take it as a compliment.

ISBN: 0-9582535-3-6

Publisher
Kingwatch Books
PO Box 21338
Christchurch 8001
New Zealand
http://www.kingwatch.co.nz

Cover Design & Layout by Tristan Brehaut for
Willson Scott Publishing Limited.
www.willsonscott.biz

Contents

There is one body and one Spirit,
one Lord, one faith, one baptism;
one God and Father of all,
who is over all and through all and in all.
But to each one of us grace has been given
as Christ apportioned it.
It was he who gave some to be apostles,
some to be prophets, some to be evangelists,
and some to be pastors and teachers,
to prepare God's people for works of service,
so that the body of Christ may be built up
until we all reach unity in the faith
and in the knowledge of the Son of God and become mature,
attaining to the whole measure of the fullness of Christ.
We will grow up into him who is the Head,
that is, Christ.
From him the whole body,
joined and held together by every supporting ligament,
grows and builds itself up in love,
as each part does its work

(from Eph 4:4-16).

CHAPTER ONE

Radical Change Required

Attaining the fullness of Christ

Promise — Jesus promised that he would build his church and the gates of hell would not prevail against it. He also promised that she would be a beautiful bride, holy and blameless before him. He prophesied that the Holy Spirit would do greater things through the Church than he had done. I believe these promises, but as I look at the modern church, something seems to be drastically wrong.

Despite some flashes of brilliance, most of our experience falls far short of what Jesus accomplished by his death, resurrection and ascension. The gates of hell are doing quite well and the Kingdom of God seems to be retreating. We are ignored by the world, left sitting in our churches crying out for revival.

The Holy Spirit has not lost his power and Jesus has not withdrawn his promises, so the problem must be at our end. I can only conclude that

> *Radical difference between the church and the world should be normal.*

our Father is unwilling to entrust the fullness of his Spirit to our wineskins (Luke 5:36-39). Modern church structures cannot cope with the blessings that God wants to pour upon us.

Desperate situations call for radical change. More of the same will not get us to where we want to be. If we want the new wine of the Holy Spirit, we must shape our wineskins according to the plan revealed by God (Ex 25:40).

Preparing for Victory — We are living at a pivotal time in history. While things are going badly for the church, the situation is even worse in the world. You don't have to be a prophet to see the dark clouds on the horizon. The kingdom of man has over-reached itself and is rotting from the inside.

Christians should not be pessimistic about the future. God is in control and is working out his purpose. He is refining his church into a holy and beautiful bride. He is shaking the nations, so his people can establish the Kingdom. We can share in that victory, if we understand his plans and get ready for battle.

The shaking of the world system will be a great opportunity for the church. In times of crisis, power flows to those who understand what is happening and are ready for action. Joseph understood what God was doing, so he was able to use the seven good years to prepare for the seven bad years. He rose to power during a crisis, because he understood what was happening and knew what had to be done.

The times are urgent. We should be using our time to prepare for the political, economic and social upheaval that is coming. We should be joining together, so we can advance God's Kingdom when the kingdoms of the world collapse and fall. Radical change is needed, so we can shine brightly in the darkness and share in the victory that God has planned.

Handbook for Radical Christians — I have put most of what I know in this book, so you may not need to read it all. Feel free to use it as a manual and grab the bits that will be useful to you. If you come to something that is not relevant to your situation, move on to something else. Chapter 3 has some radical stuff, so if you are not there yet, just skip it and come back when you are. Chapters 4 and 10 are the core that everything hangs on, so if they do not fit your situation, you have probably bought the wrong book. I suggest that you give it to someone who would be interested in it.

I have focussed on some key changes needed to revitalise the body of Christ, but none will work in isolation. They are a complete package and most will only be effective when used together. This book outlines a pattern for the body of Christ, but each Church will have to flesh that pattern out with a vision that fits their calling and situation.

CHAPTER TWO

A Different Church?

The body of Christ builds itself up in love

A Church is a group of Christians living in the same locality, who are committed to each other, who meet regularly for worship and fellowship, and who are overseen by elders manifesting the ascension gifts. There are four defining characteristics of a Church.
- Relationships
- Locality
- Elders
- Ascension Gifts

Relationships — A Church consists of a group of people who are bound together by strong relationships. These are the supporting ligaments which join and hold the body of Christ together in love, allowing it to grow up in Jesus (Ephesians 4:16). A Church is a network of people linked together by love for each other. Jesus said,

A new command I give you: Love one another. As I have loved you, so you must love one another. By this all men will know that you are my disciples, if you love one another (John 13:34,35).

Love is the essential ingredient that makes a Church unique.

Locality — The second defining feature of a Church is locality. Each Church should be attached to a particular locality and there can be as many Churches as there are different localities. Ideally, there should only be one Church in each location and each location should have just one Church. If I live in Smith Street I am part of the Church that meets in Smith Street; I am part of the body there. I do not have the option of belonging to the body somewhere else. To have a number of different kinds of church in the same locality is inconsistent with the New Testament.

Elders — Elders are the third defining characteristic of Church. Paul and Barnabas appointed elders wherever there was a group of disciples (Acts 14:22,23). Nothing more was needed to make a group of disciples into a Church. In the New Testament, a Church was a group of believers in a particular place, who were overseen by elders. Elders serve the church by:
 • Discipling Christians to maturity;
 • Building relationships between Christians.

Ascension Gifts — Every church will have elders moving in each of the ascension ministries. Each of these ministries are needed for a Church to grow to maturity (Eph 4:4-16). If any is missing the Church will become unbalanced, like a body with one limb missing.

Definition — A Church is a group of Christians living in a particular locality, who have strong relationships with each other and are led by elders moving in the ascension ministries.

For the sake of clarity, when referring to a Church, defined in this way, I will write Church with an upper case "C". When referring to a church, as it is traditionally understood, I will use lower case.

The Church in Brown Street — Imagine a group of about forty Christians, all living in the vicinity of Brown Street. They live within walking distance of each other, so they can easily visit each other, but they are not so close that other people cannot live amongst them. Despite living close together, they are surrounded by non-Christians.

People from the Church meet frequently and informally in different groups to encourage and pray for each other. Sometimes a few couples get together for fellowship or to talk through an issue. When someone faces a challenging situation, others will come round to pray for them. Different members of the group share meals regularly. They also have a lot of fun together.

Sharing — The members of the Church share their possessions. When a family has to go on a trip to another city, one of the others lends them a six-cylinder car for the journey. A few have sold their cars, having found that the need for them is gone. A couple of families have bought nine-seater vans to use when a group of people from the Church go out together. Once a week several women go out together in one of the vans to buy groceries for their families. They also get groceries for a couple of families that are busy with work. Another family has a trailer that they make available to the rest of the Church (and other people that live in the area).

Several families share the same lawn mower. Some of the people take turns at mowing the lawn for one of the others who is very busy starting a new business. At the same time they mow the lawn of an old lady who is not a member of the Church.

Joan, who is 68 years old, does not have possessions to share, but she has made her Friday and Saturday nights available to baby-sit for families in the Church who want to go out. She does not have to get up early in the morning, so she does not mind if they are late home.

Sharing is the heart of the Church. Everyone tries to own something that can be shared with the rest of the Church. They also look for opportunities to share with their non-Christian neighbours. However, sharing is always voluntary and never compulsory. People can choose not to share, but most will soon find the benefits outweigh the costs.

Leadership — The Church is led by five elders, who are very close friends. They also complement each other well. Barney is a real visionary. He sees things in black and white, so he keeps the Church going forward into God's purpose. Mark is a real open person, who loves meeting new people and has a passion for sharing the gospel. He keeps the elders from becoming a closed clique and makes sure that new people are drawn into the group.

John, Jim and Joe, the other three elders, are "people" people, who are really good at discipling new Christians. They ensure that everyone in the Church is growing and moving into their ministry. Joe's wife Jill is great at training young women who come to the Lord. Half of the women in the Church look upon her as a second mother and come to her for advice and encouragement.

Plurality of leadership is basic to the New Testament.

There is a beautiful and precious unity among the elders that is an inspiration to the rest of the Church. They have a strict agreement that no major change will be made unless they all agree to it. They also encourage and support each other in their different roles. When division comes between two of the elders, the other three work hard to restore peace and unity. If necessary, they will confront the one who needs to repent or forgive.

The elders get on very well together and it seems like nothing could come between them. However, it has not always been like that. In the early days there were many tensions, often over trivial things, that could have easily destroyed their relationship. However, they resolved early on that nothing would come between them and they have stuck to that. They have worked so hard at maintaining their unity that agreeing now seems natural.

The Church has turned out to be slightly different from what each elder expected. They each had to give up part of their vision, for the sake of unity. For example, Mark has always had a bit of a thing about Celtic music, but the others have never agreed to make it a focus for the Church. Each elder has given up a hobbyhorse, but they would all agree that the Church is better than they hoped.

No elder stands above the others or is seen as the senior elder. No one is called "The Pastor". If the people start to set one up above the others, that person quickly defers to the others. No elder tries to control or dominate the others, because they realise that they can achieve more together than on their own. They are all fairly ordinary people, but together they are a powerful team, because they support and complement each other so well.

People from other Churches often try to work out who is in charge. Some think Jim is the one, because he does not go out to work. Others think that Barney is in charge, because he is the one who speaks out the vision for the Church. Still others think that Mark is in charge, because he is the elder that they meet first. When the elders hear about this confusion, they laugh, because that is the way that they like it.

Money — All the elders except Jim work part-time. Jim has a family inheritance, so he does not need to work, but he is writing a novel in his spare time. Barney says that he goes out to work, because he gets grumpy, if he spends all his time with Christians (I think he is joking). John spends lots of time helping new Christians, so the Church tops up his income. The others don't need to receive anything from the Church. Their simple lifestyle means that they can earn enough working part-time.

The elders teach the people in the Church *not* to tithe to the Church. Running the Church does not cost much, as there is no building to maintain and no mortgage or pastor to pay. If people give too much money a problem is created and the elders have the hassle of praying about what to do with it. They prefer that people give their own money away.

No one knows how much, but the Church people give a great deal of money away. Their lifestyle means that most people earn far more than they need, so they are able to give generously. One person became a Christian when he was unemployed. A member of the Church, whom he only knew vaguely, gave him $500 on a day when his mortgage was due and his bank account was empty. He was so amazed that his heart cracked open.

Relationships — Sharing is a key feature of the Church, but relationships are the glue that holds it together. The core relationships are those between the elders. They provide a model for others to envy and emulate. They are not a closed group and their relationships extend outwards to include others.

Each member of the Church has a strong relationship with one of the elders. When a new person comes into the Church, they are discipled closely for a few months, so they grow quickly. After that intense period of discipleship is complete, the person is just watched from a distance. Each elder is watching over about ten people, so they are able to get to know them really well. They frequently share with these people in informal situations.

Undergirding all these relationships are a further set of relationships between the people of the Church. They like to have fellowship with each other, so different groups are always getting together to work on a task or have some fun.

Relationships have become so important that, some people have knocked holes in their fences to make it easier to meet. They want to stand against the spirit of the age, which is to build high fences between houses.

Relationships, like sharing, must be voluntary to be strong. People are free to choose how far they want to go in forming relationships. Several people find these relationships too intense and have chosen to remain more separate from the rest of the Church. The others understand this and still accept them as part of the Church. Standing apart is acceptable as long as the person maintains their relationship with an elder and keeps going on with God.

The elders also watch over the whole Church together. A key part of their task is to maintain unity within the Church. They move quickly to resolve any disputes. If disagreements or hurts occur, they help resolve things before people take sides and relationships deteriorate. Broken relationships strike at the heart of the Church, so their restoration is a high priority.

Growth — The Church started a little over two years ago, when Barney, Mark and Jim and their families moved into the neighbourhood and joined with a couple of Christian families who were already living in Brown Street. John was one of them. The whole group would meet to worship and pray together in his lounge.

John is one of those people who is a mate with everyone. He took Mark round to help a guy build a new deck. By the time the project was finished he had become a Christian. John then took Mark with him to meet another mate. His wife was in bed with pneumonia, so John and Mark prayed for her. She was healed and got up and made them a cup of coffee. By the end of the evening, she and her husband had also come to the Lord.

Jim spent time with John discipling these guys so that they really started to grow in the Lord. The new guys took Mark out to meet with their friends and a couple came to the Lord. They were also learning from Mark, so they soon got to the stage where they didn't need to take him, as they knew how to share the gospel themselves. Before long, they were taking others out to help them share the gospel with their friends.

The Church just kept on growing. Whenever, Jim was discipling new Christians, he always had someone with him, learning how it is done. John soon became very competent at discipling new Christians on his own, without Jim's help. Soon many people in the Church knew how to share the gospel or disciple a new Christian.

After about a year, the group was too big to meet in John's lounge. This was when Simon laid the carpet on his garage floor.

The Church has now grown to about forty adults, so the elders are talking about moving out to start another new Church. Each of them has been training up someone to take over their role. John and Joe were appointed as elders about a year ago and another three people are highly regarded in the Church. They really need the challenge of taking over from Barney, Mark and Jim, so they don't become frustrated.

The new Church will be in the next suburb, where two couples from the Church are already having an impact on their neighbours. They think that things are ready to take off in that neighbourhood. Barney thinks that one of these couples has the potential to become elders.

A Day in the Life of a Church — The people in the Church have a lot of fun together, but they are also serious about serving God. They don't have time for trivial things, so on Tuesday night many different things are happening.

In the garage of Bill's house, Bill, Joe and seven men are watching a game of football on a wide screened television. Bill does not have a car, because he lives within walking distance of his work. On the rare occasions that he needs a car, he is able to borrow one from someone else in the Church. Bill has set up a home theatre in his garage with some easy chairs, where members of the Church can get together and relax, while watching a movie or a game. Some of the children come to Bill's garage to watch television after school.

In the living room of another house, John and a couple of other men are talking and praying with a young guy who became a Christian the previous week. He has been into a lot of stuff, and by the end of the night he has been delivered from several evil spirits. In a house close by five people are praying and interceding for those doing the ministry. When someone gets a revelation, they phone those involved in ministry to pass it on.

In another house, Jill is talking with one of the solo mothers in the Church, who is having difficulty with one of her children. They agree on a strategy and commit to praying it through.

Mark and his wife are out with Dave and Dawn who are relatively new Christians. They have gone to share the gospel with Dawn's brother, who has been asking about the changes they have seen in Dave and Dawn. They have already done this before with a couple of Dave's friends, but this is the first time that they will be doing most of the sharing. Mark is only there in case they get out of their depth. Next time they will be able to go and share on their own without Mark's help.

One of the women has taken her sewing machine round to another house and is helping the owner to put up new net curtains.

The task also duplicates as a sewing lesson.

Jack, who is being groomed to take over from John, is talking with one of the new Christian men about how to deal with a job offer that he has just received. Jack makes some suggestions about a good process for deciding. They pray together before Jack goes home to make his decision.

On Wednesday night about fifteen people go out for ten-pin bowling followed by pizza. They take two couples (not Christians) who have just moved into the neighbourhood. They have a great time, and one couple really hits it off with one of the Church couples, so they make plans to go out together again next week.

> *A Church will be noticed by its neighbours, but invisible to the authorities.*

John, Jim, Joe, Barney, Mark and Jack and their wives meet together to pray about the new Church. The Lord encourages them, but they are uncertain about the timing of the changes, so they agree to wait for another month.

Persecution Proof — This Church is fairly persecution proof. Most civil authorities would not recognise it as a church, as it has no buildings, professional leaders or bureaucracy. The Church will be invisible to them, because the only regular meeting is on Sunday and it is more like a good party than a church service. The authorities would be hard pushed to stop neighbours from talking to each other or from having parties.

Victory — There is a real sense of victory in the Church. In three years it has grown to a point where it is ready to plant a new Church. Apart from the original group and Mike, all the members came to the Lord in this Church. New people are coming to the Lord all the time and some "hard nuts" have been discipled to the point where they are now real men of God. There have been some amazing healings and more than one mighty deliverance. The Church is having a powerful impact in the world.

CHAPTER THREE

Relationships and Community

There is one body and one Spirit

A church is not a building. A church is not a programme or even a Sunday worship service. A Church is a group of people bound together by strong relationships with each other. To speak of "going to Church" is missing the point. We cannot attend the body of Christ, because we are the body. We must be the body of Christ where we live.

Dry Bones — If the parts of the body are not joined together permanently the body becomes dysfunctional and the bones get dry. Ezekiel understood this very well. He saw a valley full of dry bones (Ezek 37). After he prophesied, they were joined and raised to become a mighty army. Ezekiel's vision is frequently quoted as a picture of revival, but we often miss the key point.

When Ezekiel prophesied, the bones came together and tendons and flesh appeared. The bones were joined together and skin covered them. The breath of the Spirit could not come until the bones had come together, bone to bone in a body. When Ezekiel prophesied again, the breath came into the bones and they stood up and became a mighty army.

A body is not built by throwing some bones in a basket. To become a mighty body empowered by the Spirit, the bones must be joined together. Each bone must be joined to at least two others by muscles and tendons. The correct bones must be joined in the right place. A body becomes dysfunctional, if just one bone is missing or is joined to the wrong bone.

Revival requires Relationships — Many Christians believe that revival will come as the Holy Spirit moves in power in the body of Christ. We do need the Spirit, but this is not Ezekiel's message. He warned that the Spirit cannot come in power until the body of Christ is joined together in strong relationships.

Ezekiel's message is challenging and requires radical change. We will not experience the revival we long for until the body is joined together according to God's plan (Eph 4:16). "Going to church" will not produce a revival. We cannot expect revival until we develop real fellowship based on strong relationships with other Christians.

> *Revival requires strong relationships, not going to church.*

This is a disturbing truth. If we are unwilling to be joined together in strong relationships, God's ability to send revival is severely limited. He can pour out his Spirit, but he cannot force people to connect with each other. We have to decide to make that happen ourselves. We have to choose to be the body of Christ, by committing to strong relationships with other Christians. (The full set of relationships that are needed is described in the next few chapters.)

One Another Stuff — The first step to building strong relationships is to do to other Christians the things that the New Testament requires. I call these the "One Another Stuff".

Love one another (John 13:34,35; 1 Thes 3:12 and many others).
Be devoted to one another (Rom 12:10).
Honour one another above yourselves (Rom 12:10).
Live in harmony with one another (Rom 12:16; 1 Pet 3:8).
Stop passing judgement on one another (Rom 14:13).
Build up and edify each other (Rom 14:19).
Instruct (admonish) one another (Rom 15:14).
Accept one another, then, just as Christ accepted you (Rom 15:7).

Have concern for each other (1 Cor 12:25).
Carry each other's burdens (Gal 6:2).
Forgive one another (Eph 4:32; Col 3:13).
Submit to one another (Eph 5:21).
Agree with each other (Phil 4:2).
Teach and admonish one another (Col 3:16).
Encourage one another (1 Thes 4:18; 5:11; Heb 10:25).
Build each other up (1 Thes 5:11).
Live in peace with each other (1 Thes 5:13).
Be kind to each other (1 Thes 5:15; Eph 4:32).
Encourage one another daily (Heb 3:13).
Spur one another on toward love and good deeds (Heb 10:24).
Confess your sins to each other (James 5:16).
Pray for each other (James 5:16).
Offer hospitality to one another (1 Pet 4:9).
Serve each other (1 Pet 4:10 Gal 5:13).
Show humility toward one another (1 Pet 5:5).
Have fellowship with one another (1 John 1:7).

These verses are demanding, because they require action. Doing the One Another Stuff should bring a radical change in the way we relate to other members of our Church.

Meeting in Homes — Home is the place where we like to meet with friends, so it is the best place to have fellowship. Being the body of Christ will be easier, if we go back to meeting in homes. Most Churches will meet in the lounge in the home of one of its members.

The early Christians were devoted to fellowship, so they met in their homes.

> *Every day they continued to meet together... They broke bread in their homes and ate together with glad and sincere hearts (Acts 2:46).*

Many Churches were known by the name of the person in whose house they met. We have a record of the Church in the house of Nympha (Col 4:15) and the Church in the house of Aquila and Priscilla (1 Cor 16:19). Each Church will be based in a house close to the home of one of its leaders.

In a city where the people live in apartments, Churches will look different, but the same principles will apply. The aim will be to have at least one Church in each apartment block. If a large number of people become Christians, each housing block might need several Churches on different floors of the building.

Sharing — As we learn about loving one another, we will find that love must be practical.

> *This is how we know what love is: Jesus Christ laid down his life for us. And we ought to lay down our lives for our brothers. If anyone has material possessions and sees his brother in need but has no pity on him, how can the love of God be in him? (1 John 3:16,17).*

Love is more than holding hands and singing "We are one in the bond of love". Love requires sharing with those in need. Sharing was normal in the early church, as they expressed their love for Jesus and commitment to others.

> *Selling their possessions and goods, they gave to anyone as he had need (Acts 2:45).*

Christian love produced a radically different attitude to possessions. Instead of being something to enjoy, they were seen as a gift from God to be used to strengthen the Church.

> *All the believers were one in heart and mind. No one claimed that any of his possessions was his own, but they shared everything they had. With great power the apostles continued to testify to the resurrection of the Lord Jesus, and much grace was upon them all. There were no needy persons among them (Acts 4:32-34).*

Visible Witness — Sharing is important because it makes the gospel visible. Jesus promised that if we love each other, people will be drawn to him.

> *A new commandment I give you: Love one another*
> *As I have loved you, so must you love one another.*
> *All men will know that you are my disciples*
> *If you love one another (John 13:34,35).*
> *I when I am lifted up from the earth,*

will draw all men to myself (John 12:32).
The people of the world are entitled to look at a Church to see if its members love each other. The problem is that love is not easy to see. Forgiveness and encouragement will often not be visible to those outside the Church.

The best way for Christians to make their love visible is by sharing their possessions. People who live close by will see John driving Bill's car. They will wonder why George

> *Church is something we are, not something we can attend.*

still lives in plenty, when he has just lost his job. In a world where riches and poverty are normal, a Church with "no needy people" will be a very visible witness to the love of Jesus.

Churches that are serious about doing the One Another Stuff will start sharing quite naturally. Some will share their cars; others might share part of their house with another Christian. Others will share their computers, lawnmowers, televisions, freezers, washers, power tools, etc. Every Christian will aim to have something they can share with other members of the Church.

A sharing Church would be a tremendous testimony to people living close by. Christianity is not just a personal relationship with Jesus. His death on the cross also broke down the barrier of sin that divides us from other people. His people must demonstrate their restored relationships. In a world that is hungry for love, the best witness may not be a believer saying "Jesus loves me", but a group of Christians freely sharing their possessions.

Sharing must always be voluntary. It must be motivated by love and not by peer pressure. Demanding that someone share is always unacceptable. It is a privilege, not a right.

Suburban Lifestyle — Christians who want to do the One Another Stuff face a serious obstacle. Modern suburban culture creates barriers to communication and encourages individualism. As communities are breaking down and fear is rising, high fences are going up between houses isolating people from each other.

The consequence of this isolation is that most Christians do not belong to the community where they live.

> *The early believers were all together. Modern Christians drive to church.*

Western society has been shaped by the automobile and the church has gone along for the ride. The car has brought great freedom, but we have paid a great price in loss of fellowship. Church has become something that we drive to. We usually have to get into a car to go to our home group, cell group or house church. This severely weakens the relationships between Christians, so most modern churches are almost as socially fragmented as the rest of society.

The close fellowship of the early Church was only possible because people lived close to each other. Building strong relationships is difficult, if we only meet once a week. We cannot "encourage one another daily", as the scriptures require (Heb 3: 13). The sharing that was normal in the New Testament is difficult if people do not live close to each other. For example, sharing a lawnmower is difficult for people who live far apart.

The best witness for Jesus should be the change in our lives, but for that to happen, people must see us living. At work our behaviour will be constrained by the requirements of our employer, so people really need to see us living when we are free to be ourselves. They need to see us living together where they live.

A Serious Challenge for Christians wanting more of God — Our isolated lifestyle has become so entrenched that escape seems to be impossible. However, the hard truth is that we have chosen this lifestyle; it was not forced on us by the world. We cannot control the location of our workplace, or where our interest groups meet, but we are free to choose where we live. The problem is that we have not used this freedom to strengthen our Christian fellowship.

We are free to reduce our isolation by choosing to live much closer to other members of our Church. I believe that God is calling his people to stand apart from the spirit of the age by choosing to move closer to each other. Some will respond to the call by selling their house and buying one in the neighbourhood where their Church lives. Others will knock down the fences that divide them from their neighbours.

As the world is putting up stronger security fences and shutting out the world, Christians should be breaking down the barriers and opening themselves up to others. This should not really be that hard. Christians change houses all the time, to get a better view, a better job, or a better education. Buying a house close to a group of Christian friends should not be that difficult. God's call to Abraham was much tougher (Gen 12:1). He did not even know where he was going, and he never got to own a house in Canaan.

Moving Together — Choosing to live close to other members of our Church is a different way of thinking. For most western Christians, choosing a church is totally separate from choosing a place to live. When choosing a church, we look for one with a pastor and style that we like. When choosing where to live, we try to find a locality where we can get a good capital gain or the best schooling for our children. Choosing to live in the same locality as our Church is a radical idea.

Those living in better suburbs might need to move to a less desirable area, where the entire Church can afford to live. They would be following the example of Jesus, who left his place in heaven and came to

> *Being a Christian changes how we live; it could also change where we live.*

earth, for the sake of the church. This "incarnational attitude" would counteract the "home in the suburbs" idol that dominates much of the western world.

We are called to be the body of Christ where we live, so living within a short walk of the rest of the Church should become a normal part of Christian discipleship. This will require a much higher level of commitment, but being a Christian changes *how* we live, so why should it not change *where* we live?

If those starting a new Church focus their evangelistic efforts on the location where they live, most new converts will not need to move, as they will already live close to the rest of the Church. Converts from outside the neighbourhood should be encouraged to move nearer, or helped to find a Church closer to where they live. Only the people starting the new Church would need to change location.

Moving to one location may not be practical for all Christians. The disruption caused by so many people moving house or changing church might not be worth the effort. However, living in the same location should be normal for new Churches.

Meeting in Houses may not be Sufficient — In recent years, many Christians have heard the call to start meeting in their homes. This is good, but it may not be enough. The full benefit of meeting in houses will only come, if Church members live close to each other. If we have to travel by car to get to our home meetings, strong Christian fellowship will still be very difficult to achieve.

I believe that God is calling us to be more radical than just meeting in houses. If Christians are living close to each other, it will be logical to meet in homes, but this should not be the goal. God is more concerned about how we live, than where we meet. Meeting in a house is pointless, if we have no impact on the locality where we live. On the other hand, living close together is a waste of time, if we are unwilling to commit to the One Another Stuff.

The Body of Christ on Brown Street — The Church in this map meets in a house (shaded black) near the intersection of Brown and Green Street. Most of the members of this Church live in this neighbourhood. There are fifteen houses (shaded grey) with Christians living in them. A few moved into the area, but most lived there before they became Christians.

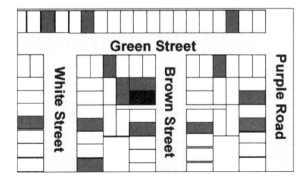

There are over a hundred houses in the neighbourhood, so the Christians have not swamped the neighbourhood. The people living among them will see Christianity in action.

Location, location, location — Church is something we are, not something we can attend. To be the body of Christ in the place where we live, we must live close to the rest of the body. Our Church should be a central part of our being, so we must belong where it is.

Each Church should be attached to a particular locality, so there can be as many Churches as there are different localities. Ideally, there should be one Church in each location and each location should have one Church. To have a number of different kinds of church in the same locality is inconsistent with the New Testament.

Benefits of Living in the Same Location — Choosing to live in the same location will enable Christians who make the commitment to develop much stronger relationships and deeper fellowship.

- Living closer together makes the One Another Stuff and a sharing lifestyle much more practical.
- Spiritual protection will be more effective if Christians are closer to each other. Those who stand alone can be picked off one at a time by the evil one.
- A Church based in a neighbourhood will provide an

environment where the radical demands of the gospel can be lived out in a simple, distinctive lifestyle.

- Strong Churches will supply an environment that supports family life through mutual support and economic sharing.
- People who have been really messed around by evil will receive intense emotional and spiritual support from Christians living around them.
- Poverty is a major challenge in many parts of the world. A Church could take responsibility for the poor in their neighbourhood and help them to climb out of poverty.
- In a hostile culture, community-based evangelism will be more successful than church-based evangelism. If there is only one church in the centre of town, most non-Christians will never go near it. By living together in the same locality, Church members will be on display in the neighbourhood where they live.
- Our dependence on the automobile is very risky. The Middle East is getting more unstable, as our dependence on it for oil increases. Every church leader should be thinking about how they will care for people prevented from driving to Church by an oil crisis.

Spiritual Strongholds — An important reason for living close together is to create a spiritual stronghold where the Holy Spirit is able to move freely. Territory and geography are really important for spiritual warfare (Dan 10:20; Eph 1:21; 6:12). To defeat the strongholds of evil, we need to establish our own spiritual strongholds.

Engaging in effective spiritual warfare is very difficult, if we only meet intermittently. Christians living in isolation from other Christians can be outvoted in spiritual warfare for their locality. Soldiers can only defend each other, if they are in constant contact.

Getting spiritual victory over an entire city is hard, as all city authorities will have to be brought in unity. In contrast, two or three Christians moving into the same neighbourhood will be able to unite in prayer to drive out the enemy.

When a locality becomes a spiritual stronghold for the Lord, the intensity of the Holy Spirit's presence will increase. People with evil in their

> *An apostolic heart will move to a new neighbourhood to build the body of Christ.*

hearts may start feeling uncomfortable and move out of the area. Healings should become more frequent and winning people for the Lord should become easier. As the number of Christians living in the area increases, the spiritual stronghold will expand.

When Jesus was speaking about spiritual warfare, he promised,

> *Where two or three come together in my name, there am I with them (Matt 18:20).*

We assume that Jesus was talking about a prayer meeting, but spiritual warfare was a lifestyle for him, so he was probably talking about a shared lifestyle.

Establishing a beachhead in a strategic locality and then expanding outward is a very effective way to take a city. An army takes a city street by street and neighbourhood by neighbourhood.

Finding the right place to start will be important. The spiritual pressure in a city is not evenly distributed, so the battle will be tougher closer to the spiritual stronghold that dominates it. The best place to start will be where the spiritual opposition is weak, such as the edge of a suburb or the spiritual boundary between two evil principalities. Christians are often heroic and rush to the toughest part of the city, whereas a wise general attacks where the enemy is vulnerable.

Jesus did not start in the key cities of Jerusalem and Bethlehem, or Tiberias where Herod lived. He built a stronghold in the fishing town of Capernaum in Galilee, where the spiritual pressure was not as intense, before pushing out to other towns (Matt 9:1). He only went to Jerusalem at the end of his ministry, when he had strong support.

Cry for Community — The need for Christian community is greatest in modern cities, where migration and urbanisation have broken down traditional community relationships. Social mobility prevents stable relationships from developing and family life is breaking down. People feel like cogs in a machine and life is characterised by loneliness and personal insecurity. In this bleak environment, people are crying out for real community.

> *A Church is a community of people living in the same locality and caring for each other within strong relationships.*

Unfortunately, most people do not see the modern church as an answer to their heart's cry. It is seen as another institution that meets personal needs with programmes run by professionals.

A Church doing the one another stuff should be really attractive to those who are crushed and alienated by the impersonality of our modern world. Love will draw people into their community.

The church has a long experience with community, but it has generally been out of the reach of most Christians. A Christian community that is only open to an elite, or requires retreat from society, is irrelevant in the modern world. We need to bring community life down to earth, so it can function in a modern city.

- Each Church should be a Christian community. Community lifestyle will be normal for all Christians, not an optional extra for superstars and misfits.
- These communities can function in any city with whatever housing is available. Special buildings are not required and there is no need to move to the country.
- No money or assets are handed over to the Church. This eliminates a problem that has troubled many Christian communities.
- Community lifestyle will be open to everyone, regardless of their personal circumstances. Anyone will fit, provided they are committed to living the Christian lifestyle in relationship with the rest of the Church.
- Christians can live as part of a community while continuing with their existing work and interest activities.
- People will be free to choose their level of commitment and what they want to share.

- People can change their level of commitment according to their stage of life. Young single people may get really involved in community and sharing. Couples with younger children may need to withdraw slightly.
- If something goes wrong with the community, people can escape by moving to another house or "walking away" from the Church. This provides protection from the domination or control that has destroyed many Christian communities.

True community can be built in a city. I can see a city that is made up of a large number of Churches that are also small communities. Each community will involve all the Christians living in a neighbourhood or apartment building. Love for Jesus will unite them together.

Christians should be leading the way and creating residential dwellings that will support a communal lifestyle. These should use resources efficiently, so that housing becomes affordable for everyone. Ironically, the only community-style housing developed by modern property developers are retirement villages for people that are "finished living", and gated communities for those who are "scared of living".

Community should not be a primary goal for Christians. Our goal is to live in total obedience to Jesus in fellowship with other Christians; community should be an unintentional by-product. The first Christians did not decide to live in community. By surrendering to Jesus and committing to fellowship they became a community by default.

CHAPTER FOUR

Leadership by Elders

*Grace was given to each of us according to
the measure of Christ's gifts*

The New Testament calls for a unique leadership model. Each
Church should be led by the Holy Spirit working through a team
of elders who are equal in status, but bring different gifts to the
leadership process. The co-ordinating and directing role belongs
to the Holy Spirit. He should be the leader of each Church.

The principle of plurality of leadership is basic to the New
Testament. Each Church should be led by several elders working
together in unity. They will submit to each other, by giving the
others permission to speak into their lives. Important decisions
for the Church will require consensus among the elders. No elder
will stand above the others.

An example of this structure is found in the Church at Antioch,
one of the most successful in the New Testament. Luke says that
in Antioch there were prophets and teachers: Barnabas, Simeon,
Lucius, Manaen and Saul (Acts 13:1). These five elders led the
Church together. There is no suggestion that one of these elders
was the overall leader.

Paul and Barnabas appointed elders in every place where there
was a group of disciples.

> Paul and Barnabas appointed elders for them in each church and,
> with prayer and fasting, committed them to the Lord in whom they
> had put their trust (Acts 14:23).

This was all that was needed to make a group of disciples into a Church. Nothing more was required. The apostles never appointed a single pastor to take charge.

The minimum number to lead a Church should be three or four. However, the number is not as important as the strength of the relationships between them. Even though the elders may have different ministries, they must have strong relationships with each other. Maintaining these relationships will be almost impossible if there are more than about seven or eight leaders.

Elders will also be maintaining relationships with six or seven people whom they are discipling. One person cannot form deep relationships with more than about twelve people. Therefore, if the number of elders increases to more than about five or six, the relationships between them will weaken and evil might sneak in.

Love One Another — Plural leadership has not worked well in the world, as sin usually gets in the way. Either, one leader dominates and takes control, or the leadership is paralysed by mistrust, division and bickering. Most Christians assume that because group leadership does not work in the world, it will not work in the church. They find it safer and easier to have one person in charge. However, the church should be different from the world.

Love is the key to making plurality of leadership work. 1 Corinthians 13:4-7 outlines a set of attitudes that will enable several Christians to lead together. Christian leaders should be free of the sinful emotions, attitudes and behaviour that divide and corrupt leaders in the world. These attitudes are not easy, but if elders cannot love one another, they cannot expect Church members to do so. Commitment to love at the top will spread love throughout the body.

The best example of this leadership style is the Trinity. The Father said about the Son, "Listen to him". However, Jesus said he could only do what he saw the Father doing. He also said it was better for him to go away, so that the Spirit could come, but when the Spirit came, he gave glory to Jesus.

Each member of the Trinity has absolute freedom and authority to exercise their perfect ministry. Yet each one honours and submits to the others. No one is in control. The Trinity demonstrates perfectly how three persons bound together by love can work together in shared leadership. To manifest the full glory of the Trinity, the church must have shared leadership.

Shared Leadership — Plurality of leadership is a serious challenge for the modern church. Having a pastor as the leader is now normal in the church. Even churches with elders have a pastor/leader. However, the New Testament never states that a Church should have "a pastor".

The hard truth is that the modern pastor/leader does not exist in the New Testament. The apostles never left one person to run a Church or singled out one elder to be a senior elder or pastor. In Antioch there were "prophets and teachers", not one pastor. The biblical model is always plural eldership (Acts 14:23, 1 Tim 5:17, 1 Tim 4:14, Titus 1:5, James 5:14). Even the apostle Paul, a mature and experienced leader, never worked on his own. He always had other elders like Barnabas and Silas with him.

When Jesus ascended into heaven, he did not leave any of the disciples as "leader". He had carefully discipled them, and taught them to expect the Holy Spirit, but he deliberately avoided choosing one person to take charge. An attempt by two of the disciples to obtain a position of precedence was strongly challenged by Jesus (Mark 10: 35-45). The Acts of the Apostles show that they did very well without a single leader, when The Holy Spirit was able to have his way.

The professional leadership model places the Christian leader under a tremendous pressure to perform that can make them feel insecure. This

> *The modern pastor/leader does not exist in the New Testament.*

insecurity is often manifested in a need to control everything in the church. The result is a vicious cycle in which pressure to perform feeds insecurity, that leads to control, that impairs performance.

A common cry in the modern church is "We need one person as leader", but this idea does not exist in the Bible, except where Samuel warned the children of Israel not to appoint a king like the other nations (1 Sam 8). He saw their cry for a leader as an expression of distrust in God and warned that it would lead them into bondage.

The desire for one man to lead is a consequence of the fall. The world has a tendency towards slavery and domination, but those who are redeemed should not have the same mindset. The church will not achieve victory with a leadership model borrowed from the world.

The Ascension Gifts — If Churches are led by teams of elders, how do the gifts of Jesus described in Ephesians 4:11 fit into a Church?

> *It was he who gave some to be apostles, some to be prophets, some to be evangelists, and some to be pastors and teachers.*

God has given the church apostles, evangelists, prophets, pastors and teachers. As Jesus gave these gifts when he ascended into heaven, they are often referred to as ascension ministries.

Much has been made recently about the restoration of these ascension ministries. Yet despite the talk, most evangelists are still in para-church organisations and few churches have a functioning evangelist. Most prophets are still in the wilderness, while very few churches have an authentic prophetic ministry. Pastors are everywhere, but very few Christians are being effectively discipled (pastored). Most modern apostles look like traditional bishops, with more of the Spirit, and less of the regalia.

Elders with Different Gifts — The most obvious way to get an understanding of the role of the ascension ministries is to read what the scriptures say they do. According to Eph 4:12-15, their role is:

> *to prepare God's people for works of service, so that the body of Christ may be built up until we all reach unity in the faith and in the knowledge of the Son of God and become mature, attaining to the whole measure of the fullness of Christ. Then we will no longer be infants, tossed back and forth by the waves, and blown here and there by every wind of teaching and by the cunning and craftiness*

of men in their deceitful scheming. Instead, speaking the truth in love, we will in all things grow up into him who is the Head, that is, Christ.

The tasks described in this passage are:
- equipping the saints for service
- building up the body of Christ
- establishing unity
- imparting knowledge of Jesus
- helping Christians to become mature
- binding the body together.

There is nothing special about these tasks. They are all things that the elders of a Church should normally be doing. This is the key to understanding the place of the gifts described in Eph 4:11. They are not of high-powered ministries or travelling consultants, but a set of tasks that elders do.

Bringing the Ascension Gifts Down to Earth — The ascension gifts are just different roles exercised by elders. This is a very radical concept, that does not fit well in our modern culture. The problem is that the cult of the superstar has moved into the church, producing a grandiose understanding of the ascension ministries.

We have made the pastor into something really big, so an apostle must be greater still. We will not accept a prophet unless he compares to Elijah. When we think of an evangelist, we think of Billy Graham. We should stop looking for the spectacular and understand that God will build his church on the foundation of ordinary people who are faithful to his calling.

A prophet is just an elder with a passion for the truth and holiness. An evangelist is an elder who has a zeal for sharing the gospel. A pastor is just an elder who loves to see young Christians grow in the faith. An apostle is an elder with enthusiasm for starting new Churches. Each elder should fulfil one of these functions, according to the gifts that Christ has given him. (One may also need the gift of organisation described in Romans 12:8).

Just Elders — According to the New Testament, the ascension ministries are just elders.

1. Some elders are apostles. The apostle John saw himself as just an elder (2 John 1; 3 John 1). The apostle Peter also called himself an elder (1 Pet 1:1; 5:1). An apostle is an elder sent out to start a new Church.

2. Some elders are prophets. Judas and Silas were elders in the church in Jerusalem. They were also prophets.

   Then the apostles and elders, with the whole church, decided to choose some of their own men and send them to Antioch with Paul and Barnabas. They chose Judas (called Barsabbas) and Silas, two men who were leaders among the brothers. Judas and Silas, who themselves were prophets, said much to encourage and strengthen the brothers (Acts 15:22,32).

   There were prophets among the elders of the church in Antioch (Acts 13:1). A prophet is just an elder with a passion for the truth.

3. Most elders are pastor-teachers. There were teachers among the elders at Antioch. Paul referred to elders who work at teaching (1 Tim 5:17). He said that elders must be able to teach (1 Tim 3:2). He also challenged the elders at Ephesus to pastor the Church of God (Acts 20:17,28). Peter also spoke of elders who were pastors (shepherds).

   To the elders among you, I appeal as a fellow elder, a witness of Christ's sufferings and one who also will share in the glory to be revealed: Be shepherds of God's flock that is under your care, serving as overseers (1 Pet 5:1,2).

   A pastor is an elder with compassion for people.

4. Some elders are evangelists. Paul spoke about elders who specialise in preaching.

   The elders who direct the affairs of the church well are worthy of double honour, especially those whose work is preaching and teaching (1 Tim 5:17).

   An evangelist is an elder with a zeal for the lost.

Prophets, evangelists and pastors are elders who care for a Church in different ways. They will use their different gifts to strengthen the people of God and to build up the whole Church. These roles should be so common that the titles are totally devalued.

The heroic leadership model comes from the Old Testament, where ministry was limited to a priestly class. Only a few people had the anointing of the Spirit, so God had to use a few great heroes. The purpose of Pentecost was to pour the Holy Spirit out on all believers. The priesthood of all believers means that everyone has access to God and can exercise a ministry for Him. We need a Church structure that allows every member to develop into a ministry or service. Rather than having a few heroes, we need millions of small ministries anointed by his Spirit.

Balanced Leadership — Each church in the New Testament was led by a team of elders (Acts 14:23). The minimum number of elders should be four or five. A Church should be led by a group of elders working together. The circles in the diagram below represent the elders. The lines represent their commitment to each other and the relationships between them. The strength of these links is the source of the strength of the Church.

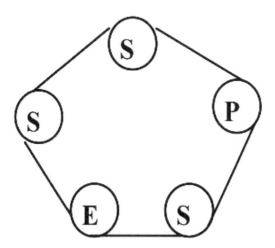

Each elder will exercise one of the ascension ministries and all of these ministries should be represented in the eldership of the Church. One of the elders will be a prophet (P). One will be an evangelist (E). Several will be pastor-teachers (S). All these ministries must be functioning together in unity for a Church to grow to maturity and unity.

Every Church must have one elder who is willing to ask the tough questions and ensure that there is an emphasis on holiness. Every Church needs an elder who has a passion for the lost and a gifting for sharing the gospel. A Church also needs elders who can help new Christians grow to maturity and ensure that all members remain united.

> *Balanced ministries are as important as plurality of leadership.*

A Church without a prophet is like a body with only one leg. A Church without an evangelist is like a body with one arm. A Church without several pastor-teachers is like a body with no heart. If any of these giftings are missing from a Church, it will be unbalanced.

These ascension ministries do not relate together naturally. Most leaders find it easier to work with people like themselves. The strength of balanced leadership comes through elders committing to work with people they would not normally get on well with.

Balanced ministries are as important as plurality of leadership. Ephesians 4 is not a description of higher level ministries or an organisational structure; it is a description of how elders with complementary, but conflicting gifts work together to strengthen the church. This is the most radical and most important idea in this book. Paul was not concerned about giving status to church leaders, but ensuring that every Church has a balanced eldership.

The simple truth is that one person cannot be Jesus. It takes at least four elders with different giftings to fully represent Jesus and accomplish his ministry.

Titles are Irrelevant — Each of these different types of service will be described more fully in subsequent chapters. For convenience I have used these titles to describe the roles, but this does not mean that a church should give these titles to its elders. If a Church has elders functioning in these different giftings, giving them titles will be irrelevant. Having an elder with a prophetic gifting is more important than calling someone a prophet.

Most elders will not want a title. They will be more interested in the maturity of the church than personal recognition. Most elders will ignore the titles and get on with serving the church using the unique gifts that God has given them.

Fourfold Gifts — The ascension gifts are often referred to as the "fivefold ministries", assuming that the pastor and the teacher are separate ministries. However, Ephesians 4:11 records that Jesus gave "some to be pastors and teachers". The construction of this expression in both Greek and English indicates that pastor and teacher is one gift or ministry. There are only four ascension gifts, because pastoring and teaching are the same gift.

The distinction between the pastor and teacher comes from a false understanding of what the New Testament means by "teaching". We tend to think of teaching as a type of preaching or a lecture to a group of students. The listeners are free to ignore what is taught.

For the early Christians, teaching was an activity involving personal direction and an exercise of authority. It took place within a relationship where the student gave the teacher authority over their life. A student would submit to a teacher, whose lifestyle he admired. His aim was to learn a way of life and the truths that support it. A teacher did not just give his views, but laid out what he expected the student to believe and the way he expected him to live. Teaching in the New Testament was more like what we call discipling or formation of character.

We can see this in the way that Jesus taught his twelve disciples. He did not just impart information to them, but developed a strong relationship with them. They chose to "follow him" and allowed him to shape their lives in a likeness of his own. Throughout the New Testament, teaching takes place within a similar relationship.

This means that the "pastor and teacher" is one ministry. Every teacher is a pastor, and every pastor is a teacher (1 Tim 3:2).

Female Elders — A tremendous variety of ministries are open to women in the Bible. The prophetic ministry was always open to women. Miriam, Deborah and Hulda are given the title of prophetess in the Old Testament. In the New Testament we have Anna the prophetess who recognised Jesus as the Messiah, when he was a baby in the temple. The four daughters of Philip are also described as having the gift of prophecy.

The apostolic ministry was also open to women. An apostle is a believer who is sent out in a missionary situation. A woman who fulfilled this ministry is Priscilla the wife of Aquila (Acts 18:1-5, 18-26). Paul met Priscilla and Aquila in Corinth, and when he went out to establish a new Church in Ephesus he took them with him. He mentions Priscilla three times in his letters as a fellow worker.

In his letter to the Romans, Paul describes Andronicus and Junia as outstanding among the apostles (Rom 16:7). Junia is almost certainly a feminine name, so Andronicus and Junia were probably husband and wife. Paul considered them both to be apostles.

In the New Testament both the apostolic and prophetic ministries were open to women, so it follows that women can be elders. Female elders are mentioned in 1 Tim 5:2. The word translated as older women is "presbuteras", which is a feminine form of the Greek word for elder. It could be also translated as elder's wife, female elder, or elderess. The passage should then read:

> *Do not rebuke an elder harshly, but exhort him as if he were your father. Treat younger men as brothers, female elders as mothers, and younger women as sisters.*

Paul is speaking of a female elder.

In marriage, two people become one, so when a man is appointed as an elder, his wife compliments him by also exercising an eldership ministry. This can be seen with Aquila and Priscilla. Because Aquila was called to be an apostle, Priscilla also became involved in apostolic ministry. Likewise Isaiah called his wife the prophetess, recognising that they had become one, and therefore shared the same ministry.

Women and Discernment — Women should be involved in the leadership process. In 1 Timothy 2:14, Paul says that it was Eve who was deceived. He was not saying that Adam did not sin, but recognising a difference between the female and male personality. Women are often more open to the spiritual world than men. This meant that Eve was more easily deceived. Adam was not deceived, but disobeyed deliberately. He sinned in a different way, because his personality was different.

Women are more open to the spiritual world, so they are often able to hear God more clearly. For this reason women should be involved in the decision making process. Eve was fulfilling a legitimate part of her complementary role in giving her advice to Adam. Her advice was wrong, but she was not wrong to give advice. Likewise, the elders of a Church should include mature women who can hear God's voice.

Deborah the Old Testament prophetess is a good example (Jud 4). Barak was the leader of the army, but he was unable to hear God. Deborah, a woman, was able to hear the voice of God. She did not take control of the army, but she advised Barak what he should do (demonstrating the correct relationship between the Church and civil government).

Rather than restricting the ministry of women, we should be encouraging them to exercise the gifts and ministries that God has given them. Women should also be encouraged to exercise their discernment for the benefit of the whole church. It can only be complete when all members are using the gifts that God has given to them. The discernment of female elders should be an important part of balanced leadership.

Qualifications of Elders — The New Testament specifies two main roles for the elders in a Church.
- Making disciples
- Building relationships

The qualifications that the Bible gives for the selection of elders are related to these functions. The elder must be holy and blameless, displaying the fruit of the Spirit in his daily life.

The main requirement of an elder is that he is able to "manage his family well and see that his children obey him with proper respect" (1 Tim 3:4). If a man has been able to build strong relationships in his family, he will be good at building relationships in the Church. If he has been able to form Christian character in his children, he will be good at discipling Christians. If he has not been able to provide spiritual protection to his family, he will be unlikely to provide spiritual protection for the Church. The early church looked at a man's family for evidence that he would make a good elder. Elders must have proved their ability by producing strong faithful families.

Elders are just people who are further ahead in the Christian life than others. The Greek word for elder is "presbuteros", which refers to someone who is older or more experienced. An elder is just a Christian recognised for their maturity by other people in the church. The title is a statement about a person's character, maturity and service to the Church.

Most Christians should be able to become elders. All that elders have to be able to do is disciple six to ten Christians, making certain that one grows sufficiently to take their place. Jesus made this clear in the Great Commission. He commanded all believers to go and make disciples. Once a person has been a Christian for about a year, they should generally begin discipling newer Christians.

Many of the problems of rebellion and apathy amongst younger Christians come about, because they are not released into ministry soon enough. There is an assumption that a person with pastoral gifts or calling must become a pastor/leader to fulfil their calling. The reality is that they can start making disciples as soon as they get their act together. When they have demonstrated ability in making disciples, they can be appointed as an elder.

Invisible Ministry — Elders should be relatively invisible. When a new person visits a meeting of a Church, the elders should not be obvious, as the leader will be the Holy Spirit. The only way to recognise the elders would be to observe the following things.

- The elders will have close relationships with many of the people in the church.
- People will be going to them for advice and assistance.
- They will not speak much, but when they do speak, everyone will listen.
- Some of the newer Christians will be imitating the way that they minister in the Holy Spirit. This is how their ministries are replicated.
- Everyone in the church will respect them for their maturity and wisdom, as many members of the church will have been discipled by them.
- The elders will have a strong sense of accountability for the Church. When something goes wrong, they will be the ones who agonise about it. They will not rest until peace has been restored.

Payment of Elders — Discipling a couple of new Christians and watching half a dozen more mature Christians should not be a full-time task, so many elders will not need to be paid. They will earn their living by working part time. Elders who are discipling a large number of new Christians with a lot of problems may need to work at it full-time, so they should be paid by the Church (1 Tim 5:17,18). Paying a couple of elders will not be a problem, if a Church does not have to pay for a building. Ten tithing families can support one family on their average income.

Hierarchical Structures — Hierarchical structures have been the norm in the church for most of its history, but it did not start that way. Jesus did not set up a hierarchy for the church before he left. In fact he objected strenuously to any form of hierarchy (Mark

10:35-38). Following his example with his disciples, the early church was structured like a family. The elders led their people in the same way as fathers care for their children.

Once the church became successful and respectable, it moved away from this biblical model towards a hierarchical model. Hierarchy has now been around for so long that Christians just take it for granted, but it has no basis in the scriptures. The Bible is the legislation of the church, so there is no need for a legislative body. The Holy Spirit is the administrator, so there is no need for administrative bodies. Where the Holy Spirit is free to work, a church hierarchy should be unnecessary. We should trust him to maintain order in the church.

Large human organisations need a hierarchy of authority to transmit information and to direct actions. Messages and instructions pass down through the hierarchy to the people on the bottom. Reports go back up in the same way. Hierarchy also allows decisions to be made at the appropriate level. The person at the top sets the general policies and rules, but delegates simple decisions down the hierarchy to an appropriate level of responsibility. Difficult or important decisions are delegated back up to the top. A hierarchical structure is very effective, but it is also dangerous, because it concentrates power in the hands of a few people.

> *The Holy Spirit is everywhere, so God does not need to work through hierarchy.*

Satan is a major user of hierarchy. He probably invented it, because he had no other way to control his empire. He is confined to one place in space and time, so he has to communicate and implement his decisions through a hierarchy of demons and evil spirits (Ephesians 6:12). His problem is that many of them are deceitful and rebellious. They disobey him frequently, so his will is not always done. When reporting about events in the world they often lie, so he is often in the dark about what is going on. Satan is at the top of a large, unreliable and unstable empire. He is a finite being, so he has to use hierarchy to control his organisation.

God is not constrained in this way. He is omniscient, so he knows everything that is happening, everywhere in the universe, all the time. He is not dependent on reports up a hierarchy. God is also omnipotent, so he has the ability to decide what should be happening in every situation in the universe at the moment it occurs. He can speak to any person in the universe, whenever he chooses, so he does not need to work through intermediaries. Therefore God has no need for hierarchy.

God does not need hierarchy in the church. He knows what is happening to every Christian all the time, so he does not need anyone to report to him. He has a personal plan for every Christian, so he does not need to delegate decisions down to a church leader. The Holy Spirit lives in every Christian, so God can communicate his will directly to any one as he chooses. He does not need to speak through a hierarchy. If every Christian obeys the voice of the Spirit, God's will will be done, without the need for any intermediaries.

There should be only two ranks in the church: Christians and elders. However, elders are not people higher in the hierarchy, who pass God's direction on to Christians below them. The role of elders is to watch over less mature Christians. They may warn them if they are being deceived or making a mistake, but telling them what to do is not their role. An infinite God can communicate his will directly to his people so he does not need hierarchy to accomplish his purposes.

CHAPTER FIVE

Making Disciples

Preparing God's people for works of service

Most Christians are looking for revival, but I believe that God will not entrust us with a large influx of new Christians until we are ready to disciple them. Too many of those who have come to the Lord have fallen away, because they were not discipled. Getting them back will now be much harder. I suspect that the Father is not willing to play this game any longer. He might be waiting for the church to take discipling seriously, before he sends revival.

Making disciples is a key task of elders. Every person who becomes a Christian should be discipled so that they grow to maturity. The heart of discipling is a relationship with an elder whose life can be modelled by the disciple (Titus 2:15).

Discipleship means learning how to be a Christian by being accountable to a mature Christian. Usually the teacher will be an elder, but sometimes the discipling will be done by other mature members of the body, with only the difficult aspects being handled by an elder.

The disciple learns in a way that is relevant to their life, as elders show them how to live the life of Christ. Elders will work in a very close partnership with the Holy Spirit and support the disciple in continuous prayer.

Discipling takes place in relationships, not in meetings. An elder must develop a strong relationship with the people that they are discipling or overseeing. This cannot be achieved through a weekly attendance at a Sunday meeting. The elder and the disciple must have regular contact and see each other functioning in real life and work situations. To achieve this they may need to be living in the same vicinity and doing some tasks together.

The elders of the Church will be very focused, so their disciples will grow very fast. When elders are spread too thin, people often do not grow.

New Christians — Every new Christian will be discipled by one of the elders in the Church. When someone joins, one of the elders will say to the others, "You look after this one" or "I'll take this one". Often the new Christian will just be drawn to one of the elders.

> *Discipling takes place in relationships, not in meetings.*

The first stage of discipling will be very intense. The new Christian will be quickly taught the basics of the Christian life. Some may need deliverance or healing. They will have lots of questions about God and his ways. The elder will teach them to experience the gifts of the Spirit and move in his anointing.

The disciple will also be taught to read the scriptures and to pray. The most important thing they will learn is to hear God speak. This will allow the Spirit to work in their life, allowing him to do most of the work (1 John 2:27).

The first few weeks of a convert's life are the most important for shaping their future, so they should be started in the way that they must go on. We are saved to obey Jesus, so a new Christian should be taught to live in obedience to him. A Christian who spends their spiritual adolescence passively listening to sermons will be hard to mobilise later in their spiritual life.

A new convert should be taught how to witness to their family and friends. The Holy Spirit will work through these relationships. For the first few times an elder (maybe the evangelist) will accompany the new Christian, to teach them how to witness. They should quickly learn to share the gospel one-to-one on their own. Within a few months they should be able to teach other Christians how to share with their friends and family.

The elder/disciple relationship should *quickly* become less intense. The basics should be covered within the first few weeks. The elder will then watch the Christian from close by. The elders may still need to answer an occasional question. The disciple may need an odd warning: "Have you prayed about that" or "What is God saying about that". Prayer covering should soon become the most important part of discipleship.

Mature Christians — Elders must be careful not to dominate the lives of their disciples. It is very easy for young Christians to become too dependent on their elders. The aim is for each Christian to grow to a level of maturity where they can walk in the Spirit and not be too dependent on an elder. The elder will then only need to *watch* from a distance, giving encouragement and correcting mistakes.

Every Christian will be submitted to an elder, but this must not be the "heavy-handed" control that has destroyed some Christians. Submission is nothing more than a willingness to let mature Christians speak into their lives. It means being teachable and willing to accept correction.

> *Remember your leaders, who spoke the word of God to you. Consider the outcome of their way of life and imitate their faith. Obey your leaders and submit to their authority. They keep watch over you as men who must give an account. Obey them so that their work will be a joy, not a burden, for that would be of no advantage to you (Heb 13:7,17).*

Submission must always be voluntary. Disciples should always be free to accept or reject the authority of the elders, so elders must not be controlling. Eldership is for protection and development, not control. Elders are servants, not rulers.

The best example of discipling by an elder is the ministry of Jesus. He chose twelve disciples and worked with them as an elder for three years (Mark 3:14). By living in close proximity, he developed strong relationships with them. Each one was given individual attention. They submitted to him and carried out all his instructions.

They gave him authority over them. This enabled him to form their lives into his likeness. At the same time he developed strong relationships between the twelve. He prepared them to work together once he was gone. In three years, they were ready to go on without him. Every elder should follow this pattern.

Replication of Ministries — A key aspect of discipling is to release the believer into a ministry. The New Testament teaches that every believer has a ministry. About a year after becoming a Christian, the elder should start guiding the disciple into their ministry. The elders must help each Christian to discern their gifts and calling and equip them for service in the ministry to which God has called them.

Elders will replicate their ministries by producing clones of themselves. This is an extremely important principle. Every elder who has developed in their ministry should be training up several people in that same ministry. In this way the ministries of the Church will multiply. Multiplication of ministry is as important as multiplication of membership.

The goal of discipling is not to produce Christians, but to release ministries. The true test of an elder's ministry is whether it is being replicated in some disciples. Jesus said that everyone who is fully trained is like his master (Luke 6:40). (In a church with one leader, this becomes a problem, as he ends up being surrounded by clones of himself).

Each elder in the diagram is shown as having people with a similar ministry close to them. Potential evangelists will tend to be drawn to the evangelist. Potential prophets will be drawn to the prophet. Potential pastors will be drawn to the pastors and start to assist with discipling even newer Christians. They will all learn everything they can from the elders they are copying. For example, Elisha was able to start where Elijah left off, because he had been well discipled by his master.

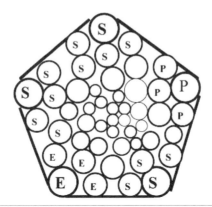

Key Points

1. The strongest Christians are on the outside. The elders are on the edge providing protection for the Church. Their protection comes through their commitment to each other.
2. The elders are a balanced team. The prophet, evangelist and pastor-teachers complement each other. They are bound together by a strong bond of love and commitment.
3. The elders are replicating their ministries in there disciple's lives.
4. The elders will work together. If one encounters a situation they cannot handle, they will call on another who has the appropriate gifts.
5. Each Christian will develop relationships with other Christians. These relationships are where the strength of the Church resides. The people are glued together by love.
6. The newest Christians (smaller circles) are surrounded by loving relationships. They will be drawn to the centre of the Church, where the love is the strongest. This is the safest place to be, as they will be surrounded and protected from the world by many Christians.
7. There is a clear distinction between being inside and outside the Church (relating to an elder). There will be no one sitting on the fence.

Restoration of Discipling — For the church to be victorious, quality discipling will have to be restored. Every elder should take a few disciples and lead them by example, until they grow to maturity. These disciples will then be able to become elders, discipling a new group of disciples. This is geometric growth. Multiplication through discipling by elders is the key to the victory of the Church.

Jesus commanded us to make disciples (Matt 28:19). He did not tell us to build a church; he will do that. He did not tell us to win people for him; that is only the first step. He told us to make disciples. Discipling is not optional, yet many new Christians are not discipled. They do not grow to maturity or develop into their own ministry. Many church leaders were not discipled themselves, so they do not know how to disciple others. This breakdown of discipleship has seriously weakened the church.

Jesus intends that all Christians grow to maturity (Eph 4:13). This will not happen by apostles directing clusters of churches, or prophets speaking anointed words at conferences, or pastors leading anointed worship services. Christians will only grow up to the fullness of Christ, if they are discipled by elders in the same way that Jesus discipled the twelve.

This changes the nature of Christian commitment. The modern way is to tell new Christians that they should be committed to a church. They are expected to express their commitment by attending a weekly meeting and tithing. The New Testament way is different. A new disciple should commit to a couple of mature Christians (elders) and copy their lifestyle. Committing to people is more natural than committing to an organisation.

The Goal — The true test of the quality of a Church is what becomes of a person who became a Christian three years earlier. If they are not functioning in a ministry (Jesus disciples were) then there is something wrong with their discipling. Every new Christian should be on a development path that will lead to a ministry within three years. The writer to the Hebrews confirmed this.

By this time you ought to be teachers (Heb 5:12).

In a quality Church this would be normal. (People who come to Christianity with severe problems may take longer to grow to maturity, but they should be on the same path).

All elders should be training someone to replace themselves, if they are called to leave. An effective elder should be able to go out to a new ministry, leaving one of their disciples to take over. If there is a balanced leadership in the Church, young pastor-teachers, prophets and evangelists will all emerge.

> *Elders replicate their ministries by producing clones of themselves among their disciples.*

Same Sex Discipling — The New Testament pattern is that male elders disciple the men and female elders disciple women. Husbands and wives should work together, so that couples disciple couples.

Paul said that women should not be allowed to disciple men (1 Tim 2:12). It would be wrong and dangerous for a woman to gather a group of men and make disciples of them, but the converse is also true. Men should not be allowed to disciple and teach women. We can see this in the ministry of Jesus. He did not choose twelve men because he considered men to be superior. He chose men because he knew it would be wrong for him to disciple women. Where men disciple women, and women disciple men, gossip and temptation follow closely behind.

Paul is saying emphatically that men should disciple men and women should disciple women. This is also seen in Titus 2:3-5 where he instructs the older women to help the younger women develop true Christian character. In a society with a lot of widowed or divorced women, it would be wrong for men to take responsibility for discipling them. Female elders should do this work.

CHAPTER SIX

Building Relationships

*Elders are the supporting ligaments that
hold the body together*

The second major function of an elder is to build relationships amongst Church members. Just as the shepherd keeps his flock together, so the elder will work to build up the whole body of believers by building strong relationships between them. A Church is a group of believers who have been bound together in strong relationships. The body must be joined together and grow by building itself up in love (Eph 4:16).

Love is not Natural — Jesus' commanded us to love one another, but love does not come naturally. The One Another Stuff is not automatic, because human nature tends to push us apart. Participating in worship and listening to sermons will not make us love one another (although loving one another may improve our worship). Christians will generally have to be taught to love each other. Teaching their people how to love each other should be a key priority for elders.

A church should be a place where Christians can learn to love each other and demonstrate the reconciling power of Jesus. He spent a large part of his ministry discipling the twelve and teaching them to love each other. Although they came from different backgrounds and had many personality clashes, he trained them to work together.

This aspect of the elder's work is clearly demonstrated in Paul's letters. A large part of them is devoted to building relationships.

Paul was not just concerned about teaching doctrine, he also taught the believers how to relate to each other. Often a whole chapter is given to strengthening his own relationship with the Church. He put also considerable energy into building relationships between people in the Churches (eg Phil 4:2). Building relationships should be a priority for all elders.

Relationships are the heart of the Church
1. The elders should have strong relationships with each other.
2. Every Christian should have a strong relationship with one of the elders in the Church, often one of the pastors.
3. Every Church member should have strong relationship with several other Christians.

The Pattern of Relationships in the Church — The foundational relationships in a Church are those between the elders. A Church will have at least four or five elders. Their relationships should be the strongest in the Church. They will be totally committed to each other. Relationships between the elders and their people are built on this foundation.

Each elder will have a strong relationship with ten to twelve people that they are discipling or overseeing. Jesus managed to disciple eleven men successfully, so it is unlikely that an elder can disciple more than ten men. If the men have wives and children, ten may be too many.

The elder in the diagram (S) has a strong relationship with about a dozen Christians. He has strong shepherding gifts, so many of the people he is discipling also have pastoral gifts.

The large circles represent Christians who are more mature. They just need oversight. The smaller circles represent new Christians who need more discipling. The lines representing the relationships are all the same thickness, reflecting equal strength. The elder will spend more time with the newer Christians to achieve the same quality of relationship. The elder will also work to establish relationships between the Christians receiving oversight.

Another elder (P) is more prophetic in his style and gifting. He will draw Christians who also tend to be prophetic. Prophetic elders will not be able to care for as many people as those with pastoral gifts, but they should still establish a strong relationship with each Christian under their care.

This elder is an evangelist (E). He tends to have a lot of new Christians around him. He is also training some more mature Christians who are keen on evangelism. This elder also builds strong relationships with and between the Christians he is accountable for.

Here are two more elders with strong pastoral gifts (S). They are each exercising oversight over about a dozen Christians. The bond between the elders draws these five groups together as follows.

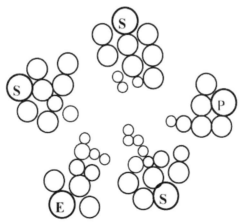

If we remember that each of the elders has strong relationships with each others, we see another dimension of the network. The relationships between the elders bring all the people together.

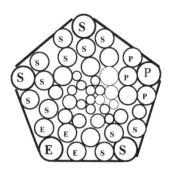

Power Pairs — The third basic relationship is the "pair". Elders also build relationships between other Christians. They will follow Jesus' example and join "pairs" of Christians together.

We all know that Jesus called twelve disciples, but we have often missed the fact that he also combined them together in pairs. In Matt 10:2-4 the twelve disciples are listed in pairs. They are also listed in pairs in Acts 1:13 (although the pairs are slightly different). Jesus sent his disciples in a pair, whenever anything significant was being done.

When Jesus sent the twelve out to preach the gospel, he sent them in pairs (Mark 6:7). Two disciples went to find the donkey for Palm Sunday (Luke 19:29). Jesus sent Peter and John together to prepare for the Passover (Luke 22:8). Prior to becoming disciples Peter and John had worked as pairs with their brothers Andrew and James.

Jesus put special effort into teaching Peter and John to function as a pair. (He knew that James and John could not continue as partners because James would be martyred (Acts 12:2)). Peter and John went up the Mount of transfiguration together (Matt 17:1). Jesus left them to pray together at Gethsemane (Matt 26: 37). They continued to work together as a pair after Jesus died (John 20:2,3; Acts 3:1,4:1,13).

The Scriptures describe many key men of God working together in pairs.
- Moses and Aaron
- David and Nathan
- Jeremiah and Baruch
- The seventy went out two by two (Luke 10:1)
- Paul and Barnabas (Acts 9:27)
- Paul and Silas (Acts 15:40)
- Two disciples on the road to Emmaus (Luke 24:13)
- Timothy and Erastus in Macedonia (Acts 19:22)

Every Christian should have another Christian who is their partner. When a person becomes a Christian and joins a Church, they should be matched up with another person to form a pair. Mature Christians should remain in a pair with another Christian. The pair is a basic relationship in a Church.

> *Two are better than one, because they have a good return for their work:*
> *If one falls down, his friend can help him up.*
> *But pity the man who falls and has no one to help him up!*
> *Also, if two lie down together, they will keep warm.*
> *But how can one keep warm alone?*
> *Though one may be overpowered, two can defend themselves.*
> *A cord of three strands is not quickly broken (Ecc 4:9-12).*

Sometimes a Christian will be a member of more than one pair. For example, Peter was in a pair with Andrew his brother. He was also in a pair with John, while John was also in a pair with James. Some people may belong to two or three pairs. These overlapping relationships will link pairs together, so if the pairs are strong, the whole body will be strong.

Over time the pairs may change. For example, Thomas started with Matthew, (Matt 10:2) but finished in a pair with Philip (Acts 1:13). We do not know the story behind this, but the Holy Spirit had a purpose in changing the way the pairs worked together.

Many soldiers, fighting together in a war have learned the importance of being part of a pair. Mates can watch out for each other by doing everything together. Surviving an intense battle together strengthens the bond between them.

The Role of Pairs

- Two Christians praying together in unity have authority to change things in heaven (Matt 18:18,19). We have lost some of the power of prayer, because most praying is done in groups and too few are praying in pairs.
- Pairs will serve the Lord together. Two men who trust each other will achieve far more together, than they can achieve separately. If John had got out of the boat with Peter, he may not have sunk in the water.
- A pair of Christians who are committed to the Lord will stir each other along. If Peter had taken John into the courtyard with him, he may not have denied Jesus.
- When Christians are sent out into a new work, they should be sent out in pairs. When Jesus sent his disciples out, to preach the gospel, he sent them out "two by two". He knew they would spur each other on and have confidence to try things together that they would not normally do. When Peter and John worked together a lame man was healed.
- A pair of Christians will provide spiritual support for each other. If one is under spiritual pressure the other will pray for him. Two people supporting each other have real spiritual protection. When King Saul fell into sin, his friend Samuel cried out to God all night (1 Sam 15:11). We all need this type of friend.
- A pair of Christians will often be discipled together. In addition to building a relationship with God, they will be taught to relate to each other.
- The power of the pair will help prevent Christians falling into sin. If one is making a mistake, the other will be able to correct him. When King David fell into adultery, his friend Nathan came and confronted him (2 Samuel 11,12). We all need someone who knows us well enough to see through our pretence.

Commitment is the key to developing a pair. The best way for two men to become a pair is to work together on a task. The tougher the task the stronger the relationship will become. Preaching the gospel together or some activity where they confront evil together will really strengthen the pair. That is why Jesus sent his disciples out two by two. For women, pairs will be established more by talking and providing emotional support for each other.

Building relationships takes time. Sometimes a pair may choose to live in houses next to each other, so they can work together more effectively.

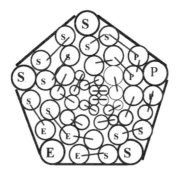

A key role of elders is to build the members of their church into pairs that can work together effectively. Often the people who need to be joined for the strengthening of the body are not naturally drawn to each other (eg potential pastors and prophets). Elders will identify people who have complementary ministries and get them supporting each other. They will ensure that the various parts of the body are fully joined together according to God's plan.

Special Anointing on Pairs — Matthew 18:20 is quoted frequently, but we have failed to notice what Jesus was really saying.

> For *where two or three come together in my name,*
> *there am I in the midst of them.*

"Two or three" is taken as a quorum, the minimum number needed for Jesus to be present. This is true, but Jesus was saying much more. He was saying that "two or three" is the best relationship. The Holy Spirit loves working with two or three Christians who are really committed to each other. The full power of God will be with them. Therefore, two or three people coming together in Jesus name is as good as it gets.

We miss Jesus' point, because in our hearts, we really believe that Jesus' presence is greatest in a really large meeting. One hundred is good, but a thousand is better. However this is not true. The power of the Holy Spirit does not get divided up between Christians, so it is not multiplied if more Christians are present. In fact, because there is likely to be less unity in a large group, his power will often be diminished.

Joining the Body — A body is not built by joining each part to every other part. Rather it is built by every part being perfectly joined with the part of the body that is next to it. If the foot was slightly joined to the eye, the hand, the head and the backside, the body could not function. The foot must be perfectly joined to the leg, to fulfil its function. When the foot is joined to the leg and they function as a pair, the body can walk freely. The connection to the leg is more important than the relationship with any other part of the body.

Every Christian must have a special relationship with one or two others who can support them in their ministry. If we really want to know the presence of Jesus we must get together in twos or threes and seriously do the one another stuff.

Every believer should be in a relationship with one or two other Christians who can provide:
• A warning when taking the wrong path (Col 3:16).
• A challenge to besetting sin (James 5:16).
• Support when standing against demonic attack (Jam 4:7).
• Encouragement in ministry (Heb 3:13).
• Comfort when things go wrong (2 Cor 1:4,5).

Network of Relationships — A Church is a group of people who are bound together by strong relationships. To show this more clearly, I will remove the people from the diagram (this is for illustration, I am not saying that they are unimportant).

A Church is a network of relationships. The lines on the diagram are just some of the relationships that hold the Church together. They are the supporting ligaments which join and hold the body of Christ together in love and allow it to grow up in Jesus (Ephesians 4:16). Elders build their church by ensuring all these relationships remain strong.

Measuring Success — Numerical growth is not a true indication of success. A truly successful church is one where strong relationships are being formed. This will happen easiest in a smaller church. In a large church, those in the "inner circle" will have strong relationships, but many people will participate in the church's activities without getting to know anyone very well. They can get lost on the fringes. In a church where relationships are strong, no one will be able to hide, as the elders will notice and join them into the Church.

Dandelion Model — In the dandelion model most relationships are through the pastor. This can make a church very fragile. If the pastor leaves, falls away or is arrested, the relationships are weakened because the pivot is gone. Unless the pastor is quickly replaced, the church can easily fall apart. This has been a frequent occurrence in recent years. A new pastor has often struggled to bring all the church back together again. In the network model, if one elder falls away, the other elders can quickly close the gap and the rest of the church will be kept safe. The only ones who will be lost are those totally loyal to the fallen elder.

Hierarchical organistaions are becoming obsolete in the modern world.

The hierarchical form of organisation was useful in traditional societies for providing order and control, but it tended to stifle creativity and spontaneity. In the modern world, this level of control is no longer acceptable and the world is shaking off the bonds of hierarchy. Networks are replacing hierarchies. A strong network allows a group of people with diverse skills and talents to co-operate in a highly effective and productive way.

The business world is rapidly transitioning from hierarchy to networks as modern information technologies reduce the costs of communication. Decision-making is being decentralised and the development of business networks has increased the efficiency of many business processes. Despite these trends, the church is still very strong on hierarchy and control. To be effective in the modern world, the church will have to transition from the dandelion model to a network model.

An Asian Tale — Zhang Yesui lives on the tenth floor of a government housing building in a large Asian city. The Church that meets in his apartment started about a year ago, when two men and their families moved into flats on the floors below. They had been sent out from a Church in a building on the other side of the transit station.

The new Church really got under way when Wang Ran, a young girl with a crippled leg had been healed. Everyone who lived in the building knew her. They would see her coming back to her flat, struggling to manage her packages and her crutches. The two men had prayed for her and she was instantly healed. She was so overjoyed that she gave her heart to Jesus.

The limp was gone and her face glowed with joy, when Wang shared the good news with Zhang's wife. Zhang and his wife soon became Christians too. The two apostles started a Church in the Zhang's flat with Wang and another girl from the same building.

The Church has grown so fast that the flat is now a real squeeze. Sometimes 35 people squash into their living room, with the surplus overflowing into a bedroom. All the space on the floor is taken up and a few of the younger people only have standing room. They often run out of air, but the presence of the Holy Spirit just seems to get stronger. Every time they meet something happens. Many people have experienced healings and there have been some powerful prophecies.

On a fine day they sometimes meet in the park around the corner from their building. Wang Ran will text the members of the Church and tell them where to meet. The old people sit on the park benches and the young ones sit on the paving. The park is so crowded that they are hardly noticed, but a few other Christians join them.

Chapter Seven

Pastor-Teacher

Jesus gave some to be pastors and teachers,
so we become mature

Most elders will be pastor-teachers. The word translated as pastor in the New Testament is the Greek word for shepherd. It is mostly used as a verb, describing the work (pastoring) of elders.

From Miletus, Paul sent to Ephesus for the elders of the church.... Keep watch over yourselves and all the flock of which the Holy Spirit has made you overseers. Be shepherds of the church of God, which he bought with his own blood (Acts 20:17,28).

To the elders among you, I appeal as a fellow elder, a witness of Christ's sufferings and one who also will share in the glory to be revealed: Be shepherds of God's flock that is under your care, serving as overseers–not because you must, but because you are willing, as God wants you to be; not greedy for money, but eager to serve (1 Pet 5:1-3).

The phrase "be shepherds" is a verb in the Greek, so pastoring is something that elders do.

Except for real shepherds and references to Jesus as the Great Shepherd, the word "pastor" is only used as a noun once in the New Testament. That one instance is in Ephesians 4:11, where the pastor-teachers (plural) are part of a shared leadership team. Therefore, "pastor" is not the title of a church leader, but the role of an elder.

Pastor is not a title of a leader. Pastoring is something that elders do.

A shepherd is a person who cares for a flock of sheep. He leads them to a place where they can find food and water. He keeps the flock together, so it is safe from attack. At the same time each sheep receives individual attention and those that stray are brought back to the flock. Each one is known by name and any sick sheep is healed.

The elder who is a pastor and teacher has four key functions.

• Making Disciples
• Restoring Broken People
• Building Relationships
• Providing Oversight

The pastoral ministry is very important for the growth of the church. The section on pastoral ministry in this book is quite short. This is not because it is not important, but because it not my area of expertise (the observant reader will have noted that I do not have the gift or calling of a pastor). Fortunately, there is plenty of good teaching on this topic by others who are really good shepherds.

1. Making Disciples — The first task of the pastor-teacher is making disciples. Every Christian must be helped to grow to full Christian maturity, as measured by the stature of Christ. As a shepherd feeds his sheep, a pastor-teacher will teach Christians how to grow to maturity.

Most discipling will be done by elders who are pastor-teachers. Evangelists will be more occupied with preaching the gospel, than developing new Christians (unless they have an urge to evangelise). Prophets tend to have very high expectations of their disciples, with the result that they can easily be crushed. They will be more focused on developing holiness and vision in the whole Church as a group.

Prophets will have a role in discipling potential prophets, and evangelists will assist with discipling potential evangelists. From time to time, every member will need the ministry of a prophet willing to confront besetting sins. The evangelist will encourage all church members to witness for Jesus.

2. *Healing Broken People* — An authentic Church must have room for people who are crushed and broken by life.

> *The LORD is close to the brokenhearted*
> *and saves those who are crushed in spirit (Psalm 34:18).*

Apostles are often so focussed on building the next Church that they become intolerant of those people who need a lot of care. Prophets have high standards and get frustrated with those who cannot attain them quickly. Evangelists are good at seeking the broken-hearted, but they usually do not have the patience to help them sort out their lives. Pastor-teachers will have the compassion and patience to put time into those who are brokenhearted or wounded, allowing them to grow at their own speed.

Elders with a pastoral gifting add an important balance to the leadership of a Church. Apostles, evangelists and prophets all tend to be very task focussed. In contrast, pastors always put people first. Good pastors will not use people to fulfil their vision, but will give their lives for their sheep.

From time to time, the pastors will need to remind the other elders that people are more important than progress. They will give a lead in doing the "one another stuff", because it is natural to them. The ministry of the pastor-teacher is vital, because they ensure that the Church demonstrates the love and grace of Jesus.

3. *Building Relationships* — The third function of the pastor-teacher is to build relationships among Church members. Just as the shepherd keeps his flock together, so the elder will work to build up the whole body of believers.

Elders who are pastor-teachers will take most of the responsibility for keeping the Church united. Prophets tend to be more concerned about holiness than unity. The abrasive side to their character can cause division. Evangelists are usually too busy seeking the

> *Building relationships will be a priority for elders with a pastoral giftings.*

lost to be concerned about unity. Most of the burden for building relationships will fall on the elders who have a pastoral calling.

4. *Providing Oversight* — Pastor-teachers provide spiritual protection by "watching over" the Church. Even mature Christians need a relationship with a pastor-teacher who will challenge them if they are being deceived and pray with them if they are being attacked. The word "oversight" describes this relationship well, because the pastor-teacher "watches over" the believer.

Paul described the role of the elders and pastors of the church in Ephesus.

> *Keep watch over yourselves and all the flock of which the Holy Spirit has made you overseers. Be shepherds of the church of God.... (Acts 20:28).*

The Holy Spirit had made them overseers of a flock. Paul challenged them to guard their flock. They do this by *watching over them* to see that they do not come to harm. Mature Christians do not need to be closely discipled. They just need someone to watch over them, to intervene if things go wrong. Jesus bought them with his blood, so they must not be allowed to slip away.

In the New Testament, elders are often referred to as overseers. The words "elder" and "overseer" are used interchangeably in Titus 1:6,7 to describe their ministry. Oversight is not a different role, but is a key task of elders with pastoral gifts.

The word translated as "overseer" is "episkopos". "Skopos" means "watch" and "epi" means "around", so "episkopos" describes watching over or around. Pastor-teachers "watch over" the disciples that God has placed under them. Some versions of the Bible translate the word "episkopos" as "bishop". This is misleading as it makes an overseer sound like an administrative position. Overseeing is not controlling, but watching over mature people to see that they remain safe.

Peter also challenged elders to exercise "oversight" by serving and setting an example, not by ruling or controlling.

> To the elders among you.... Be shepherds *of God's flock that is under your care, serving as* overseers.... *being examples to the flock* (1 Pet 5:1-3).

Elders watch over their people like a shepherd watches his sheep.

A good shepherd does not force his sheep to eat and grow. He finds good feed for them and they eat and grow naturally. He just watches that no sheep are straying or pushing the others about and that no thieves or predators are attacking. He leaves the growing to the sheep. The best example of a pastor watching over his disciples and providing spiritual protection is Jesus. He "protected them and kept them safe" from evil (John 17:12).

Spiritual Protection — We are involved in a spiritual battle, so the Christian life is very dangerous. Life in wartime is very different from life in peacetime. Soldiers on a battlefield must be alert at all times and always ready to defend themselves. Spiritual warfare is not something that we can choose to do; we are engaged in it all the time.

Despite being engaged in a spiritual battle, many Christians do not know how to defend themselves against evil. Some go over the top and see evil spirits everywhere, and others just ignore evil. The result is that many Christians are weakened or defeated by the forces of evil. We need a more balanced understanding of defence from evil.

A modern army would not send soldiers into battle without teaching them how to defend against attack. In the same way, pastor-teachers should train Christians how to defend themselves from evil. Their main task is to watch over the Church to ensure that it is protected from evil. Pastor-teachers have a key role in the spiritual protection of the Church (1 Pet 5:1-9).

Evil Attack — Deception is Satan's best weapon. God has made us free agents, so we have control over our lives. Satan cannot force us to sin, if we refuse, but he can persuade us to sin by putting thoughts into out minds to justify wrong actions. By getting us to believe that something evil is good, or to accept a distorted view of God, he hopes to open us to sin. If we take ownership of these thoughts and give them a home in out hearts, they will begin to affect our behaviour and actions. For example, Adam and Eve sinned when the serpent persuaded them to question God's words (Gen 3:1,4).

Incorrect thoughts are more effective if they are associated with strong emotions, like anger or fear. Deceptive thoughts will often come into our minds at a time when we are emotionally stressed. To produce this stress, the devil can use other people to attack us, eg persecution, opposition, slander, robbery etc. These attacks cannot make us sin, but they will often produce the emotions that make us susceptible to negative thoughts.

When we constantly accept a pattern of false ideas, it becomes a mental stronghold that Satan can exploit at will. If we listen to a false idea a number of times, it becomes part of our memory. This also happens if we identify with it strongly, or it is associated with strong emotions. Once the thought is in our memory, Satan no longer needs to put it into our mind. We will bring it out ourselves, whenever we are in a similar situation or feel the same emotions. The thought has become a mental stronghold that controls part of our thinking and influences our behaviour (2 Cor 10:4,5).

Satan's second best weapon against Christians is to afflict our bodies with pain and sickness (Job 2:7). Job was a righteous man yet Satan had the power to touch him (Job 2:3). Epaphroditus was attacked with sickness to prevent him from doing the Lord's work (Phil 2:25-27). Sickness weakens people and makes them less effective in service of the Lord. It also produces negative emotions that make them vulnerable to false ideas. Inflicting sickness is very effective in the western world, because Christians do not associate sickness with Satan.

Resist Evil — Resistance is the key to dealing with evil attacks (including sickness). James said,
   Resist the devil, and he will flee from you (James 4:7).

We should not ask God to deliver us, but resist the evil directly ourselves. Paul gave the same advice.

> *Put on the full armor of God so that you can take your stand against the devil's schemes…. put on the full armor of God, so that when the day of evil comes, you may be able to stand your ground, and after you have done everything, to stand. Stand firm then…. (Eph 6:11,13).*

We are told to "stand" four times in this passage. The Greek word translated as stand is "histemi". It means to stand, stand firm, make a stand or hold one's ground. The word translated as "resist" is the Greek word "ant-histemi", which literally means to "stand against". Resisting is the same as standing. Resisting the devil is important for spiritual protection.

Standing with other Christians — Standing against evil is not something that we can do on our own. The word "stand" is plural in the Greek New Testament, so we must stand together with others to achieve victory against a concerted attack. The spiritual armour is ineffective when standing in isolation. The shield of faith cannot cover our backs, so full protection comes through being in relationship with other Christians.

Healthy relationships with other Christians provide a key to spiritual protection. If we start to accept false ideas from the devil, they will begin to affect our behaviour and influence our decisions. If we are

> *Resistance in unity with other Christians is the key to dealing with an evil attack.*

being deceived, we will not be aware of it, but our close friends will notice the change in our conversation and behaviour. (It may be possible to fool the elders, but it is very hard to fool your friends).

Our friends should love us enough to honestly challenge the false ideas that we are being tempted to accept. As they challenge these false ideas, they will also resist the devil in prayer and release the Holy Spirit to speak the truth. We should all give a pair of trusted Christian friends the right to challenge us, if we are being deceived or making wrong decisions.

Sickness is tough to deal with. We often cannot resist it standing alone. It is hard to have faith, when burdened with sickness, so resisting becomes difficult. We need others to stand with us and do battle. If we are under attack by sickness, we usually need others to stand and resist with us.

A sick person does not have the energy for spiritual battle. Our faith tends to weaken, when we are weak or unwell. In this situation we need Christian friends who are full of faith, who can stand against the evil attack with us and pray for our healing.

The paralysed man had friends with faith in the power of Jesus to heal (Luke 5:18). That was a good situation to be in. In contrast, the man beside the pool had no friends to press in for his healing (John 5:5-7). Spiritual protection from sickness comes from being in relationship with Christian friends, who will go into battle, whenever we are attacked by sickness. If one member is sick, the entire body is weakened (1 Cor 12:26). Christian friends committed to resisting attacks of sickness with us are the best protection against sickness.

Christian Elders — The support of Christian friends will be adequate to deal with most attacks. However, we may need the intervention of mature pastor-elders to assist against really serious attacks. For example, anyone who seriously loses the plot will need correction from elders. In some situations, we may listen to an elder, when we will not listen to a friend.

Pastor-teachers may have greater discernment than other Christians. If the attack is clever, we will often not realise that we are being attacked. The best protection is a good relationship with an elder who can see what is happening and give a warning.

When operating in unity, elders will have greater power in prayer against deception. Elders can really do spiritual battle for us, because they will have the full range of giftings needed to deal with any situation.

We will also need pastors to deal with the really tough attacks of sickness. The pastor-teacher will stand and resist with the sick person.

Is any one of you sick? He should call the elders of the church to pray over him and anoint him with oil in the name of the Lord. And the prayer offered in faith will make the sick person well; the Lord will raise him up (James 5:14,15).

The elders should have the power and authority to blow sickness away.

Keys to Personal Protection

We face two main types of personal attack from the forces of evil:
- Deception
- Sickness

Protection from deception comes from:
- Christian friends who love us enough to honestly challenge any false ideas that we are tempted to accept.
- Elders to correct us if we seriously lose the plot.

Protection from sickness and disease comes from:
- Friends who are full of faith who can stand with us and pray for our healing.
- Elders who can pray for tough cases (James 5:14).

If we do sin, we need:
- A friend who has authority to challenge us
- An elder who will warn us if we don't listen.
- A friend who will pray against deception
- Elders who can really do spiritual battle for us, if we get hooked.

Submission is Essential — Submission is very important for effective resistance of evil. When we submit to each other, we are giving other Christians the authority to act on our behalf against evil. This is a key to getting victory. God has made me free, so another person can only have authority in my life, if I give it to them. I give another person authority in my life by submitting to them. If I submit to the elders in my church, they have authority to resist evil on my behalf. The more I submit to them, the greater spiritual authority they will have to resist any evil that is attacking me.

This relationship between spiritual authority and submission is not well understood. We often ask other Christians to pray for us, but it does not have much affect. The reason is that they have very little authority in our lives; but they cannot have authority, if we have not given it to them.

We often assume that if we have a large number of people praying for us, their prayers will be more effective against the attacks of the enemy. This is not correct. When resisting evil, two or three Christians who have real authority in our lives, because we have submitted to them, will be much more effective.

Spiritual armour is only effective when we are resisting together in submission to each other. The meaning of the word "submit" is to "place ourselves under". Therefore we must stand under authority before we stand against the devil. Submission and authority go together.

When Paul said that elders watch over or care for us (1 Tim 5: 17), he used the Greek word "pro-histemi", which means "stand before". When we submit to elders, they are standing before us.

According to the pattern in 1 Peter 5:5-9, submission and protection go together.
  • Submit to one another
  • Submit to your elders
  • Submit to God
  • Be vigilant
  • Resist the devil
  • Stand in the faith

Dangerous Pyramid — Having one person as leader of a church is spiritually dangerous. Spiritual authority and protection comes through submission to authority. If one man leads a church, all the church members submit to him. This gives the pastor/leader tremendous authority, but leaves him vulnerable to satanic attack and deception. Most Christian groups that have gone haywire, were led by one person.

True protection comes when a group of elders all submit to each other. Each elder is accountable to the others and protected by this submission. The members of the Church are then protected by submitting to their elders.

Spiritual Protection of a Church

1. Each Church should be led by a team of elders who submit to each other for protection from evil. If one falls the others will raise him up. It is unlikely that all would fall at the same time. The elders have strong relationships with each other. Their unity is strength.

2. An elder is watching over each Christian and covering them with prayer. Each member is submitted to the elders. This gives them protection from any fall that would make them vulnerable to the devil.

3. The elders are a balanced team. The pastor-teachers deal with hurts or relationship problems that could cause problems. The prophet challenges false ideas and rebellion that could sneak in.

4. The people of the Church are submitted to each other, so they have authority to do battle for each other. If a person is attacked by evil, his friends have the authority to stand together with him in prayer. If a person falls into deception or sin, his friends will challenge him before too much damage is done. He will accept their correction, because he knows that they love him.

5. If the friends cannot get victory, they can call on the elders for help. The elders are looking outward, resisting the devil. They stand united against him (James 4:7).

6. Living in the same location is important for spiritual protection. If a Church can establish a spiritual stronghold in the locality where they live, getting victory over evil will become much easier.

Christians are being decimated by evil and too many leaders have fallen into immorality or been struck down by sickness, because they do not have adequate spiritual protection. This has been painful for them and their families. It has also done tremendous damage to the church and harm to the gospel. The fact that so many good men have fallen is a sign that something is wrong with the spiritual protection that the church is providing for its people.

Qualifications of Pastor-Teachers — The qualifications of pastor-teachers are determined by their role. They will need strong people skills, balanced with the gift of discernment. Pastor-teachers will do a lot of discipling, so they will need experience in teaching new Christians. They should have the ability to get on with all types of people and see the best in them. Pastor-teachers should be good at building strong relationships between diverse people. They will be experts on the "one another stuff".

The elders have an important role in protecting the church from sickness, so they should have gifts of healing in their midst (James 5:14,15). To be recognised as a pastor, a person will need to have proved that they have the ability to deal with sickness. They should have demonstrated this by resisting sickness in their household/family, before being appointed to the position of elder.

The passage on qualifications of an elder in 1 Tim 3:5 says that an elder will "care for the church". The Greek word translated as "care" is only used in one other place in the New Testament. The Good Samaritan used the same word when he asked the innkeeper to "care" for the wounded man until he was well (Luke 10:34,35). This suggests that a person should not be appointed as a pastor-teacher if they do not have victory over sickness in their family.

When David was a shepherd, he dealt confidently with a bear and a lion. He did not just chase them away, but killed them so they would not attack again. Pastor-teachers are not wimps. They should be tough enough to deal with evil with the same confidence as David.

Restoring the Pastoral Ministry — I believe that the pastor/leader model, so prevalent in the modern church, has created a desperate shortage of pastoring. The problem is that many pastor/leaders are not true pastors at all, but unfulfilled apostles, or businessmen who have not found their calling in the Kingdom of God. A genuine pastor cares too much about people to have the drive needed to lead a large organisation. They simply do not have the toughness and energy to be a modern leader.

The result of inadequate pastoring is that only a fraction of new Christians are fully discipled and even fewer move into a ministry. Many churches are full of half-done Christians. Large numbers of Christians get lost and fall away each year. This problem is so serious that we now take it for granted that many new Christians will fall away, despite the fact that Jesus did not lose any of the people entrusted to him (John 17:12).

When Jesus saw the people suffering from sickness and disease, he was filled with compassion for them (Matthew 9:35,36). He saw them as being harassed by Satan, like

> *The pastor/leader model has created a desperate shortage of real pastoring in the modern church.*

sheep without a shepherd (pastor). I suspect he looks upon many sick Christians today and sees them as harassed and without a pastor. He wants to send them shepherds, who will not preach at them, but see they are healed. The most urgent need in the Church is for pastors who can set their people free from sickness. True pastor-teachers will have both the compassion and the faith needed to get the sick healed.

Most pastor/leaders are wonderful, dedicated, loving, enthusiastic people, but they are spread too thin. A weekly sermon, a monthly chat and a program once a year will not defeat evil attacks and transform lives. The inevitable result is a few very exhausted pastor/leaders, far more frustrated potential pastors, and a large number of immature and defeated Christians.

Challenge — Ezekiel 34:1-4 is a strong word to church leaders. The prophet does not criticise them for shortage of anointing, or lack of vision or inadequate management and organisation skills.

His concern is that the shepherds are neglecting the following tasks:
- Caring for the flock
- Strengthening the weak
- Healing the sick
- Bringing back the strays
- Searching for the lost

These are the things that Peter and Paul challenged pastor-teachers to do.

Many voices are saying that God is restoring the apostolic and prophetic ministries. That may be true, but I believe that the greatest need is for the restoration of a true pastoral ministry to the church. Considering the large numbers of Christians who remain immature, and the equally large number who fall from the faith, we urgently need God to restore the ministry of the pastor to the eldership of the church.

The Army — An army is not trained by gathering all the soldiers, from generals to privates for two hours a week and spending the first 30 minutes singing battle songs and the next hour listening to a general lecturing on tactics and the history of war. This would make a very ineffective army.

Soldiers need to learn discipline, obedience and weapon skills. These skills are learned by doing drills. They are not fully trained until they are battle hardened. Most soldiers are not trained by generals, but by NCOs. The generals concentrate on tactics and planning.

CHAPTER EIGHT

The Prophet

Jesus gave some to be prophets
so we will not be tossed to and fro

The Prophetic Voice — The restoration of the prophetic ministry is essential for the vitality of the church. In recent years the gift of prophecy has been rediscovered, but there is still a desperate shortage of prophets. The church will not come to true maturity until God has raised up prophets among his people. Prophetic elders are urgently needed in our time.

Lack of vision and direction causes many Christians to float from fad to fad, with none followed through to completion. Many churches are weak in vision and only obtain one by copying other successful churches.

The Bible says that without a vision the people will perish (Prov 29:18). A dearth of prophets has caused a lack of vision in the church. Paul says,

> If the trumpet does not sound a clear call, who will get ready for battle (1 Cor 14:8).

The Church needs prophets who can give this clear call to battle. We are surrounded by a great babble of voices, all claiming to have the truth, and many Christians are tossed around by every new wave that comes along. A clear prophetic word is needed to prepare the church for victory.

Prophets will bring the guidance of the Lord to the church. Christians can get so caught up in the events of the world that they do not see what God is doing. In tumultuous times, the hand of God can be hard to see. Prophets will give direction and vision in these situations, so that Christians will know what God is doing, and what they should do. For example, the prophet Gad provided guidance to David and showed him how to avoid trouble.

> *But the prophet Gad said to David, "Do not stay in the stronghold. Go into the land of Judah." So David left and went to the forest of Hereth (1 Sam 22:5).*

Reliable Prophets — In recent years we have seen an increase in the manifestation of the gift of prophecy in the church. This has been a great blessing to the church, but much of the prophecy that is given is rather tame. This is not the way it should be. Paul said:

> *if an unbeliever or someone who does not understand comes in while everybody is prophesying, he will be convinced by all that he is a sinner and will be judged by all, and the secrets of his heart will be laid bare. So he will fall down and worship God, exclaiming, "God is really among you! (1 Cor 14:24,25).*

Prophecy with this power is not common in the church. Jeremiah said that the word of the Lord is like fire, or like a hammer that breaks a rock in pieces (Jer 23:29). The church will only experience powerful prophesying, when prophets are given their proper place.

Prophets in the Church — We should not be looking for heroic prophets like the men of the Old Testament. The outpouring of the Holy Spirit means that this gift has been distributed far more widely (Acts 2:17,18). We should be praying that God will raise up numerous prophets to take their place in balanced eldership teams. Every Church should have a prophet with a true ministry to speak the word of the Lord when it is needed.

A prophet is just an elder who sees things in black and white. Having this ministry present in the eldership will help the Church grow to maturity and unity. Prophetic elders will keep the Church on the right track and ensure that there is an emphasis on holiness.

They will ask the tough questions and challenge Christians with besetting sins. A prophet is an elder with a passion for truth and righteousness.

The prophetic ministry is a fundamental aspect of the eldership.

Now you are the body of Christ, and each one of you is a part of it. And in the church God has appointed first of all apostles, second prophets, third teachers, then workers of miracles, also those having gifts of healing, those able to help others, those with gifts of administration, and those speaking in different kinds of tongues (1 Cor 12:27,28).

Every Church needs at least one assured prophet. Sometimes it can be difficult to test a prophecy, because the message given is rather general.

> *A prophet is just an elder who sees things in black and white.*

The prophecy may be biblically correct, but it may not be what God is actually saying at the time. It is more fruitful to test prophets. They can be watched over a period of time to see if their lives bear fruit. Jesus said that this is the best test of a prophet. A false prophet will soon become obvious through the damage that is done by their ministry (Matt 7:15-20).

Payment of Prophets — A prophet's loyalty to God must take priority over their loyalty to the Church. While being sufficiently involved to know what is going on, they must be detached enough to be objective. This means that a prophet should not be paid by the Church.

Paul says that gifts of money should only be given to those elders who work hard at teaching or preaching (1 Timothy 5:17). Pastor-teachers and evangelists can receive financial support. Prophets are not included, because being a prophet is generally not a full-time work. They can work part-time to support themselves. An example of this is Amos, who earned his living as a shepherd. If a prophet is financially independent he will not be tempted to compromise.

Pastors and Prophets — Every Church needs both prophets and pastor-teachers. The two ministries are complementary, but they have not always fitted together well. Pastors tend to be warm loving people. This is the strength of their ministry, but it means that they can sometimes find it hard to confront evil. They love to see people grow and to see the Church united, so they can be tempted to compromise for the sake of peace and unity.

Prophets have a zeal for holiness and truth that balances this tendency. And whereas pastors tend to concentrate on the present, prophets can give vision for the future. On the other hand, prophets have zeal for purity and righteousness that can make them appear hard and harsh. Pastors will temper this with love and grace.

The reason there is a lack of prophets in the modern church is that they are led by pastors and the bluntness of the prophet does not sit easily with them. If the pastor is insecure, he can be hurt by the prophet's words. The prophet seems to be a nuisance and life is easier if they leave.

As the modern church is led by pastors, the prophetic ministry will only be restored to the church, if pastors allow it. I believe that many pastors have (sometimes unwittingly) obstructed the restoration of the prophetic ministry in the church. This has prevented God from doing all that he wants to do. Sometimes pastors are hostile or fearful of the prophetic due to bad experiences, but this is not an excuse for robbing their people of what the prophetic ministry can bring to their church.

> *Pastors and prohpets
> working in unity
> reflect the love
> and holiness of God*

Although pastors may be concerned about the damage done by immature prophets, the reality is that controlling pastors and inadequate pastoring have done far more damage than over-zealous prophets. Pastors have far more power over people's lives than prophets, so a pastor who gets lost can do real harm. In numerous situations, a whole church has fallen when their pastor has lost the plot.

Pastors have a key role in encouraging the development of the prophetic ministry. If they want to fully serve God, pastors will have to deal with the prophetic (and its problems). The church will never reach its full potential without the ministry of the prophet, but the prophetic ministry will only be restored in God's fullness, if there is a radical commitment from pastors to make it happen.

To fully represent Christ, the church must exhibit both the love and the holiness of God. Love without holiness is compromise. Holiness without love is harshness. If pastors and prophets are present in a Church, then holiness and love will both be evident. The Church will be a true reflection of the character of God.

Establishing Prophets in the Church — Most churches have no prophet to establish holiness and righteousness. They do not have a mature prophet to disciple budding prophets, so God has had no choice but to develop prophets in the wilderness. This is a second best option that produces lots of problems, but is the only way, until the prophetic ministry is fully restored to the church.

Pastors can take the initiative to restore prophets to the church. Those from a church with no prophet should look in the wilderness for a growing prophet and seek to establish him in their church. Obadiah protected, fed and sheltered the prophets when Jezebel was trying to destroy them (1 Kings 18:3,4). There is an urgent need for Obadiahs in our time.

Pastors should encourage those in their church with prophetic gifts to grow in their ministry. They will then have prophets in their midst who can be trusted to speak the Lord's word. The more that pastors encourage the prophets, the better they will perform. Prophets respond to listeners. By exercising discernment, pastors can help prophets to hear the word of the Lord.

Who should be in Charge — A serious argument about authority is going on in the church. Some people say that prophets do not need to submit to anyone, but God himself. Others say that everyone including the prophets must submit to a pastor. Still others say that apostles will govern the church and that pastors and prophets will both submit to the apostles. All these views are wrong. The Bible is quite clear.

Submit to one another out of reverence for Christ (Eph 5:21).

Apostles, pastors, prophets and evangelists are not above this command. They are required to submit to each other out of reverence for Jesus.

Instead of asking who is to govern and who is to submit, we should be looking for a model of church government that allows all the ministries to submit to each other, as required by Ephesians. Arguing about who should be in control will only result in division and disunity.

> *The modern church has millions of pastors, but only a few prophets.*

Restoring prophets to the church will not work, if pastors attempt to control the prophets. The challenge to the pastors is to say to the prophet, "We will submit to you, if you will submit to us". They will both have to trust each other by submitting to each other. This will be risky for both the pastors and the prophet, but if they commit to it out of love for Jesus, great blessing will follow.

Trust produces trust and responsibility. Pastors will be surprised at how responsible prophets can be, if they are just trusted. Prophets will be surprised at how open pastors can be, if the prophet is willing to submit to them.

Paul started in his ministry when Barnabas found him and brought him to Antioch (Acts 11:25,26). Barnabas demonstrated great courage, because Paul was a high-risk person, but his trust brought out the best in Paul. His commitment to Paul released enormous blessing into the church.

Every Church needs several pastors, at least one prophet and at least one evangelist to function effectively. There will only be unity if they are all submitted to each other. The prophet should submit to the pastors, but the pastors should also submit to the prophet.

Pastors, prophets and evangelists are very different from each other and are likely to have strong views about how things should be done. A great deal of love and trust will be required for them to submit to each other; but this should be normal for mature ministries. If the cross of Jesus is at work in their lives, it will be possible for these ministries to submit to each other.

Mutual submission amongst pastors, prophets and evangelists will be good for the Church. Their unity will provide balance and safety for the Church. It would also be a marvellous testimony to the power of the gospel. On the other hand, if pastors and prophets cannot submit to each other, then there is something wrong with our gospel.

Many church leaders are concerned about their members lack of submission, yet they are unwilling to submit to others themselves. If the leaders of the church cannot submit to each other, then we should not be surprised if there is a lack of submission among less mature Christians.

Developing Young Prophets — Developing young prophets can be a real challenge for pastors. When first starting their ministry, prophets are often negative and over-critical. Their intolerance and insensitivity can be very irritating to the pastors, causing them to come down hard on the prophet at the first mistake. The young prophets are often so crushed that they do not dare to prophesy again.

The problem is that, because prophets are sometimes negative and hard in their words, pastors assume that they must be dealt with severely. They do not realise that under their brusque exterior, most prophets have a very sensitive spirit that can be easily broken. They need a great deal of encouragement if they are to develop into their full ministry.

At the same time, young prophets must learn to be patient, and allow God to develop their ministry. This will take time. Daniel was just a young man when he arrived in Babylon. He was middle aged when he received his first vision, and quite old when he received his greatest visions. Jeremiah was still prophesying when he was an old man.

Young prophets only have partial vision. At times they will speak the Lord's word in the wrong spirit. God will allow them to make mistakes, to humble them. They should not grasp at ministry, but wait on God to raise them up in due time. Those who humble themselves will be exalted.

Young prophets will not emerge properly in a church that is led by a pastor alone. (The same applies to evangelists). Pastors cannot disciple budding prophets effectively. The young prophet will either start challenging the pastor and become disruptive, or he will be stifled by the pastor and lose his cutting edge. A young prophet will develop best in a church where mature pastors and a prophet are in submission to each other. He will be drawn to the prophet and will learn how to function in the prophetic from him. He will also learn how to relate to pastors.

A young prophet will need frequent and firm correction. This will generally be better received from a mature prophet whom he respects. However, when he is treated harshly by the older prophet or becomes discouraged, as often happens, he will also need and appreciate the comfort and encouragement of a pastor. Young prophets need healthy relationships with both pastors and prophets. If they can grow within these relationships, they will be less likely to wander off into bitterness and isolation.

Welcome True Prophets — Churches must be careful not to quench the spirit of prophecy.

> *Do not put out the Spirit's fire;*
> *do not treat prophecies with contempt.*
> *Test everything. Hold on to the good.*
> *Avoid every kind of evil*
> *(1 Thessalonians 5:19-22).*

The words of all prophets should be weighed carefully. The Scriptures give clear guidelines for testing prophecies. Anything that is good should be received; the rest should be discarded. Prophets can be uncomfortable people to have around. They can often be hard to take. We must avoid taking offence at their style and manner and missing what God is doing through them.

Prophet to the Nation — The primary responsibility of a prophet is to bring direction and correction to their Church, but God calls some to be a Prophet to the Nation. Many of the prophets of the Old Testament found themselves confronting kings, and taking an important role in national affairs. Some also addressed their words to foreign nations.

A Prophet to the Nation releases God's hand of power. We are living in a time of transformation, when God's purposes will be accomplished through "shaking" and judgement. The ministry of the prophet is very important at these times, because God cannot act, without first giving a warning through his prophets.

> *Surely the Sovereign Lord does nothing without revealing his plan*
> *to his servants the prophets (Amos 3:7).*

God cannot shake a nation until he has announced it through his prophets. There are two reasons for this.

i) God is merciful and always gives people an opportunity to repent, before he sends judgement on a nation. He would be happier if he did not have to shake it, so he gives a warning, hoping that people will turn around. But if the warning is not heeded, God has no alternative but to act himself.

ii) Any shaking event must be recognised as coming from the hand of God. If a judgement is seen as just a normal event, it can be ignored. An event that has been announced beforehand by God's servants is obviously a work of God and its meaning will be clear. The fact that it has been announced beforehand by God's servant will be proof that it is a work of God.

In the troubled times that lie ahead many people will have their hope shattered. The plans and the projects to which they have given their lives will collapse. Often they will feel as if God has abandoned them. The nations will need prophets who can give new vision in these times of shaking. They will explain how God is at work in what appears to be a disaster. And because prophets can see what lies ahead, they will be able to give hope for the future.

Speaking for God — A Prophet to the Nation speaks on behalf of God. Peter said that the prophets were carried along by the Holy Spirit.

> *Above all, you must understand that no prophecy of Scripture came about by the prophet's own interpretation. For prophecy never had its origin in the will of man, but men spoke from God as they were carried along by the Holy Spirit (2 Pet 1:20,21).*

The prophets were moved by the Spirit, so they could speak in the name of the Lord.

When calling Jeremiah, God said he would put his words in the prophet's mouth (Jer 1:7,9). The same point is made in Deuteronomy 18:18:

> *I will raise up for them a prophet... I will put my words in his mouth, and he will tell them everything that I command him.*

Prophets should only say what God tells them to say.

> Most prophets will function as an elder in a Church and only a few will go on to be a Prophet to their nation.

Prediction of the future is important for the Prophet to the Nation. Almost every prophet in the Old Testament first appeared as a foreteller. Through their fellowship with the eternal God, prophets have access to the future. They are the seers with insight into God's purposes for history. However, what they see for the future is always related to the present. Prophets warn of future judgements, so that people will change their behaviour. They speak of future blessing to give hope for the present. The prophets speak to the present, in light of the future that God has revealed to them.

Prophets admonish, warn, direct, inspire, encourage, intercede, teach and counsel. This ministry is well described in Jeremiah's challenge to the false prophets:

> *But which of them has stood in the council of the LORD to see or to hear his word? But if they had stood in my council, they would have proclaimed my words to my people and would have turned them from their evil ways and from their evil deeds (Jer 23:18,22).*

A Prophet to the Nation must spend time in the presence of the Lord. When they know the heart and mind of the Lord, they must speak the word of the Lord to the nation or its leaders. The prophet stands before the nation as one who has stood before God. Prophetic words from the heart of God are powerful and effective. They are especially effective in turning the leaders of a nation away from sin.

Prayer is an important task of the Prophet to the Nation. Because they know the mind of the Lord, they are in a position to pray effectively. They have a clear picture of what God is doing, so they know where prayer is needed most. Prophets must watch over the word of the Lord, and pray it into being. They must not rest until God has fulfilled his word (Isaiah 62:6).

Calling — The initiative in raising a prophet up from their Church to speak to their nation always rests with God. This is not a ministry that anyone can take up, so it will be quite rare. Only false prophets dare to take up this ministry for themselves. The true prophetic ministry always begins with a call from God (Jeremiah 1:4-10; Isaiah 6:1-8).

The proof that a prophet has been called to speak to the nation is the fact that their words are effective and fulfilled. For example, all of Israel knew that Samuel was a prophet, because the Lord was with him and let none of his words fall to the ground (1 Samuel 3:19,20).

A calling to speak to the nation will be rare. Most prophets will function as an elder in a Church and only a few will go on to become a Prophet to their nation. We should not confuse these two roles. Most prophetic people will never get beyond the ordinary role of elder in their Church. Those with a ministry in a Church should not presume to be a Jeremiah or an Amos.

Prophetic Attitudes — All prophecy must be delivered with the right attitude. The truth must be spoken in love; an incorrect attitude nullifies the truth of a word. Many true prophecies have been made false, because they have been spoken in a harsh or critical attitude.

Once the word is delivered, the prophet's task is finished, except for prayer. Prophets must leave the results to God. A prophet, who nags in support of a word, quickly loses credibility and detracts from the word. A prophet should deliver the word in the right way in the right attitude and leave God to do the rest.

A Prophet to the Nation must be a servant of God's word, whose only concern is that the word be heard. Prophets must avoid the trap of pushing their name forward. This pushiness often comes from frequent rejection, but must be resisted. If the word is heard, the prophet can be forgotten.

Prophets are human, so this is easier to say than to live. When a prophet hears a word he brought being quoted, his heart will often scream for *his name* to be mentioned. This feeling is human, but is dangerous for the prophet, because it is rooted in pride and pride kills prophecy. Prophets must struggle to quiet their hearts and be content if the word they spoke is being heard and accepted.

Every prophet must learn to deal with rejection, because rejection is normal for prophets.

> *Blessed are you when people insult you, persecute you and falsely say all kinds of evil against you because of me. Rejoice and be glad, because great is your reward in heaven, for in the same way they persecuted the prophets who were before you (Matt 5:11,12).*

All prophets will experience times when their words are not accepted and obeyed. If this happens frequently, the prophet can become frustrated, and frustration can lead to bitterness. Words spoken out of frustration and bitterness will be contaminated by these things and will not come out pure. Rejection is the most *serious* problem faced by prophets. They must learn to deal with rejection without going into frustration and bitterness.

Prophets see things in black and white, so they must also be careful not to take on a critical spirit. They are vulnerable to the spirit of the Pharisees, whose blindness to their own sin made them over-critical of others. A critical spirit can add a harshness to

> *The truth not spoken in love is not the truth.*

a prophet's words, even if their basic theme is true. A prophet who enjoys giving hard words almost certainly has a critical spirit.

False Prophets — Whenever God brings forth a ministry, Satan will bring forth a counterfeit. That should not put us off, but make us careful. If we hear that counterfeit money is in circulation, we do not stop using money. We just become more careful. As the prophetic ministry grows, false prophets will become more prevalent. We should not reject prophecy, but be vigilant. Elders should guard against false prophets by ensuring their Church has a fully developed prophetic ministry. True prophets are the best antidote against false prophets.

Jesus warned that false prophets would come as wolves dressed in sheep's clothing.

> *"Watch out for false prophets. They come to you in sheep's clothing, but inwardly they are ferocious wolves. By their fruit you will recognise them. Do people pick grapes from thornbushes, or figs from thistles? Likewise every good tree bears good fruit, but a bad tree bears bad fruit. A good tree cannot bear bad fruit, and a bad tree cannot bear good fruit (Matt 7:15-18).*

False prophets are not always obvious. At first they appear to be credible. However if they are allowed access to the flock, they can do terrible damage.

The Bible has strong warnings for false prophets (Ezek 13:1-12; Jer 6:13-15; 14:11-16; 23:16-18).

> *They have lied about the Lord; they said, "He will do nothing! No harm will come to us; we will never see sword or famine. The prophets are but wind and the word is not in them; so let what they say be done to them" (Jer 5:12,13).*

Good News Prophets — In Old Testament times, the most serious problem was the "court prophets". They were part of the establishment and acted as cheerleaders for the King, whether he was obeying God or doing evil (1 Kings 22). The modern equivalent is the "pet prophet" who is so loyal to his pastor/leader that he "barks on command". Prophets must be careful not to become part of the establishment. They must find their security in God. Micah had a serious warning for "good news" prophets.

> *This is what the Lord says: As for the prophets who lead my people astray, if one feeds them, they proclaim 'peace'; if he does not, they prepare to wage war against him. Therefore night will come over you, without visions, and darkness, without divination. The sun will set for the prophets, and the day will go dark for them. The seers will be ashamed and the diviners disgraced. They will all cover their faces because there is no answer from God"* (Mic 3:5-7).

Prophets who only give positive messages are dangerous. In the modern church, there are far too many "comfort prophecies" and not enough prophecies that have come out of the council of God. Despite the apparent sophistication of our age, we live among a highly gullible generation that is open to false prophets and false messiahs.

The Watchman — A watchman was standing on a watchtower. He saw trouble coming and told the shepherds to get the sheep into the safety of the fold. The shepherd asked the watchman to get the sheep into the fold. However, when the watchman tried to round up the sheep, they just scattered. They did not know the voice of the watchman. Only when the shepherds heeded the watchman's warning and called the sheep did the sheep come into the fold.

Prophets are watchmen. They stand on the walls of the city of God so that they can see what God is doing and call the people to respond. Watchmen look out into the darkness and the distance to see what evil is coming and what God is doing. Good relationships between pastors and the watchman are essential. The watchman should communicate what they see to the pastors. The pastors can then prepare the sheep for what is going to happen. The sheep know their shepherds and they will respond to them.

CHAPTER NINE

The Evangelist

Jesus gave some to be evangelists, so the body will grow

Some elders will be evangelists. An evangelist is an elder who specialises in preaching the gospel. They will go out from the Church into the world, to preach the gospel and draw people in. At the same time they will lead and train others in evangelism. Philip exercised this ministry, so Luke described him as "the evangelist" (Acts 21:8).

Qualifications — There are three criteria for selecting a person for this ministry. First, they must demonstrate the fruit of the Spirit in their life. They will also have a good understanding of the gospel of Jesus Christ. An evangelist must be able to answer the questions that are raised by enquirers (1 Pet 3:15). Finally, they must have demonstrated that they are able to proclaim the gospel successfully. The main sign that a person is being called to be an evangelist is that many people are being won for Christ by their preaching.

Evangelists will be outgoing people who feel at home in the hurly burly of the market place and the public square. They will take the gospel into any place where people are meeting; into the taverns and onto the streets. True evangelists are always aggressive, not waiting for sinners to come to them, but going to any place where they gather. Their greatest joy will be to see a large crowd listening to the gospel message.

A deep love for the lost will motivate all their actions. They will often weep for those who refuse to accept the gospel. Their love will be obvious to all who hear their words. Signs and wonders will often accompany their preaching, as a visible demonstration of God's love for those who are in bondage to the devil. Evangelists must be experienced in the gift of healing and ministry of deliverance.

At the same time, there will be a toughness about the character of an evangelist. Brawling crowds or anti-christian authorities will not intimidate them. Their zeal for the gospel will be so strong that they will not be deterred, even if the authorities forbid the proclamation of the gospel (Acts 5:27,28,40-42). They will often act like a prophet when confronting rulers who obstruct the gospel. A good example of this is Stephen, who under the inspiration of the Holy Spirit, gave a stern warning to the Jewish authorities who had arrested him for preaching (Acts 7). Evangelists will not be frightened to confront sin and will boldly warn of its consequences.

Evangelists and the Church — Most professional evangelists have had to work in para-church organisations, because they have not found a place in the church. Those who have found a paid role in the church have usually been forced to become pastor/leaders. In this role they may win many converts, but they do not have the pastoral abilities needed to disciple them.

Evangelists who pastor churches tend to use evangelistic methods. They care for their people by preaching at them, because this is the gift they have. In-depth ministry is often done

> *Good preachers should be sent out into the world where preaching with signs and wonders belongs.*

at the front of the church after an "altar call". This kind of ministry tends to produce thrill-seeking Christians, who are dependent on their pastors and big churches with immature people.

Evangelists should be freed from their pastoral duties, and sent out into the world, where preaching with signs and wonders belongs. They should be freed to develop the full potential of their ministry. Every Church should have at least one evangelist who can go out into the world and preach the gospel and teach others to do the same.

Not every Christian is called to be an evangelist, but we are all commanded to be witnesses. Every believer must be prepared to give an answer to anyone who asks about their hope, as they go about their daily life. Every believer must be a witness to Jesus.

Most evangelism will be done by new Christians. A key role of the evangelist will be to teach new converts how to witness to their family and friends. The first few times they do it, the evangelist will accompany the new Christian. They should soon learn to share the gospel on their own.

Healing and Evangelism — Healing of the sick is essential for effective evangelism. The gift of healing is mainly for unbelievers and not for Christians. Jesus came to save the lost and when he was healing the sick, he was ministering to unbelievers.

Jesus destroyed the power of sickness and sin, so there are no limits to his authority and power. He healed:
- all diseases (Matt 4:23),
- all people who came to him (Matt 12:15), in
- all places (Luke 9:6).

Jesus authority has not changed (Heb 13:8) and he has given the same authority to his disciples.

Jesus method of evangelism was to visit a town and pray for the sick.

Jesus went throughout Galilee, teaching in their synagogues, preaching the good news of the kingdom, and healing every disease and sickness among the people (Matt 4:23).

When a crowd gathered to see what had happened, he would preach his message (Luke 6:17-20). The healing confirmed Jesus' message by demonstrating the power and compassion of God.

Jesus gave the same commission to his disciples (Matt 10:7,8).

When Jesus had called the Twelve together, he gave them power and

authority to drive out all demons and to cure diseases, and he sent them
out to preach the kingdom of God and to heal the sick (Luke 9:1,2).

The New Testament pattern is:
• receiving authority,
• preaching the gospel,
• healing the sick.

We have the same authority to preach the gospel and to heal the sick. Jesus promised that,

These signs will accompany those who believe: In my name they will
drive out demons...... they will place their hands on sick people,
and they will get well." Then the disciples went out and preached
everywhere, and the Lord worked with them and confirmed his word
by the signs that accompanied it (Mark 16:17,18,20).

Jesus promised that God would confirm the preaching of the gospel by the signs and wonders that accompany it.

Peter and John experienced this as they went to the temple and God healed a lame man. An amazed crowd gathered so Peter preached to them. Several thousand were saved, because God gave authority to Peter's words before he had even spoken. The same was true for Paul and Barnabas.

Paul and Barnabas spent considerable time there, speaking boldly for the
Lord, who confirmed the message of his grace by enabling them to do
miraculous signs and wonders (Acts 14:3).

The Holy Spirit loves to confirm bold preaching of the gospel with gifts of healing and deliverance.

Normal New Testament evangelism is based round the healing of the sick. This is confirmed in Acts 8:5,6:

Philip went down to a city in Samaria and proclaimed the Christ there.
When the crowds heard Philip and saw the miraculous signs he did, they
all paid close attention to what he said.

The passage says that the Samaritans were amazed at the miracles, but only that Philip preached the gospel. Luke just assumed that proclaiming the gospel includes healing and miracles.

Our good news is that God is merciful, but a cynical world does not believe our claims. Healing demonstrates God's mercy and proves that Jesus is the saviour. The best visual aid for the gospel is someone who is visibly sick being healed (the other is baptism).

Evangelism Strategy

1. Evangelists should be led by the Spirit to a place where God has prepared people and wants to do things. This will usually be a public place where a crowd is likely to gather. Jesus was always in the right place at the right time (John 5:19).
2. Once in the right place, the evangelists should then identify the person that the Father wants to heal. The Holy Spirit will point him out. When Jesus went to the Pool of Bethesda, he chose the paralysed man out of the great number of sick people waiting by the pool (John 5:3). He was the one that the Father wanted to touch. Sometimes the person will come to the evangelists. The lame man at the gate of the temple, came to Peter and John asking for money, but the Holy Spirit wanted him healed (Acts 3:3).
3. Having identified the person that God wants to heal, the evangelists should lay hands on them and pray for them to be healed in the name of Jesus. If the Holy Spirit has indicated that he wants the person to be healed, he will do what he said he would do and make the person whole.
4. When the person is dramatically healed, a crowd will gather. An evangelist will take the opportunity to preach to the crowd. They will explain that the healing is a demonstration of the grace of God and the power of the gospel.
5. The evangelist must be prepared to pray for all people who come seeking healing. When they see what the Holy Spirit can do, many will come looking for God to touch them. They will be looking for God's mercy, so he will not disappoint them (Mark 1:30-34, Acts 28:8,9).
6. All who respond to the gospel should be baptised.

Public Places — We all want to see the Holy Spirit healing the sick, but we often forget where it happens. Here are two passages that provide a key to successful evangelism.

And wherever he went–into villages, towns or countryside–they placed the sick in the marketplaces. They begged him to let them touch even the edge of his cloak, and all who touched him were healed (Mark 6:56).

As a result, people brought the sick into the streets and laid them on beds and mats so that at least Peter's shadow might fall on some of them as he passed by (Acts 5:15).

Large numbers of people were healed in the streets and the market place. This is where the Holy Spirit loves to work. He loves to go into the public places and heal the sick. If we want to see him doing this, we should follow him (Matt 10:6).

Modern Evangelism — Most modern evangelistic campaigns are very different. The evangelistic meeting is often held in a church building, so a powerful publicity campaign is required to get people to attend. The evangelistic method is worship, sermon and altar call. These methods do not exist in the New Testament.

New Testament evangelism is healing the sick, casting out demons and preaching to the crowd that gathers. This method was very successful for the early church, so we are unwise to do something different. Sickness is the key vulnerability of the modern world. Our affluent lifestyle has given people almost everything they need, but modern medicine has not been able to conquer sickness and pain. A gospel confirmed by healing of the sick will be well received by the modern world.

Jesus said,

I am going to send you what my Father has promised; but stay in the city until you have been clothed with power from on high (Luke 24:49).

If we do not have the power that we need for New Testament evangelism the answer is simple: we should wait until the power from on high comes to us (see also Acts 1:4,5). I suspect that God would prefer that we do some serious waiting, so that we can do evangelism his way, rather than rush into doing evangelism our way.

Going to the lost with the gift of healing is very important. Over the last few decades God has been restoring the gift of healing to the church, but we have tended

> *The Holy Spirit will go to the lost without us, if we do not go with him.*

to keep it in the church and only pray for Christians. This is a mistake. Jesus said the sick need a doctor, not the healthy (Luke 5:31).

Praying for Christians is a good way to learn about healing, but we need to move on to healing the lost. If we do not, we will tend to lose the gift. The Holy Spirit loves the world and is always moving out towards it to draw people to the Father. If we do not go with him, he will go on without us, leaving us empty.

Altar Calls and Baptism — Modern evangelistic methods are based around a sermon followed by an altar call. However, there were no altar calls in the New Testament. Raising a hand or signing a card is not an adequate response to the gospel. Baptism is the biblical response to the gospel.

Baptism should take place as soon as possible after conversion. This was the practice of the New Testament church.

- Those converted on the day of Pentecost were baptised on that very day (Acts 2:41).
- The Philippian jailer was baptised at midnight on the same night as he received the gospel (Acts 16:33).
- The Ethiopian was baptised as soon as he and Philip came to some water (Acts 8:38).

Baptism is a testimony that a person has become a Christian. It is a clear sign to everyone that they have left their old life and joined the Kingdom of God. Baptism is also the means by which they receive the Holy Spirit (Acts 1:38). It completes the work of the evangelist.

Deacons — The ministry of the deacon is the other major evangelistic thrust of the Church. Some evangelists will start their ministry as deacons. Philip and Stephen both began their service as a deacon and then went on to a successful ministry as an evangelist.

This forgotten ministry needs to be restored. In the New Testament, deacons cared for the poor. They were the "social welfare arm" of the Church. The record of the appointment of the first deacons is in Acts 6. Men like Barnabas, when called to a Christian ministry, had sold their property and "brought the money and laid it at the apostles feet". The twelve used this money to provide for those in need.

When the number of disciples had increased, some of the Grecian Jews complained because their widows were being overlooked in the daily distribution of food.

> So the Twelve gathered all the disciples together and said, "It would not be right for us to neglect the ministry of the word of God in order to wait on tables. Brothers, choose seven men from among you who are known to be full of the Spirit and of wisdom. We will turn this responsibility over to them and will give our attention to prayer and the ministry of the word (Acts 6:2-4).

This proposal pleased the whole group so they appointed seven men who were full of the Spirit. They presented these men to the apostles who laid hands on them. The result was that the word of God spread, and the number of disciples in Jerusalem increased rapidly.

If we love those we are helping, we will be prepared to go and live among them.

The deacons were responsible for the offerings of the Church. They used them to provide for the needs of the poor and the sick. In doing this they were fulfilling the parable of the Good Samaritan. When he found a person in trouble, he took action to meet the immediate need. He then took further action to find a permanent solution, taking responsibility for the cost himself. This is a good pattern for the ministry of a deacon.

Qualifications of Deacons — The qualifications for the selection of deacons are listed in 1 Timothy 3:8-13. These are relevant to the nature of their work.

1. A deacon must be a person who does not pursue dishonest gain. Because they are responsible for the money of the

Church, deacons must be trustworthy. They must have proved that they can handle money wisely and responsibly.

2. Second, a deacon must be able to manage his household. If a man cannot manage his own household, then he will not be able to manage the finances of the Church. The elders should look at the way a person's household is functioning for evidence that he has the ability to do the work of a deacon. However, there is another reason why household management is important. The deacon also has a teaching role. He does not just give money to the people who are poor. He also teaches them how to manage their households better, so that they can manage on their own in the future. A deacon could not do this unless he was skilled in managing his own household.

3. A deacon must also have a clear knowledge of the truths of the faith. This is because he also has an evangelistic ministry. The Christian gospel is always directed to the whole person. If a person is hungry, it is no use preaching the gospel to them, without feeding them. On the other hand, feeding a hungry person is no use without doing something about their spiritual needs. Deacons have a total ministry to the poor. As they distribute food and clothing, they will also preach the gospel. This is why they must have a good knowledge of the faith.

4. People skills are more important than knowledge of finance and administration. The early Church chose deacons who were skilled in working with people.

5. Deacons should be full of the Spirit (Acts 6:2-4). They will need the discernment and wisdom that only the Holy Spirit can give.

Female Deacons — Women can fulfil the ministry of the deacon. Deaconesses are referred to twice in the New Testament. Phoebe a deaconess of the Church of Cenchrea is mentioned by Paul in Romans 16:1. The women referred to in 1 Timothy 3:11 are almost certainly deaconesses.

The ministry of the deacon can be performed well by a married couple. The husband would work with men and his wife would work with the women. The deacon's wife would concentrate on helping the wives to manage their homes wisely.

Widows can also exercise this ministry. They would have responsibility for caring for the other widows in the Church. Where a Church is under persecution this would be a very important ministry, as there will be many widows or women with husbands in prison.

Women tend to function better than men in situations where personal care is needed. Female behaviour is often orientated towards helping and caring for personal needs. This means that women often do the work of a deacon better than men. They should be released into this ministry.

Problem and Opportunity — One of the problems faced by deacons in the modern world is that their function has been taken over by the state. The modern social welfare state gives cradle to grave security for its citizens. The result is that deacons have been left with nothing to do but care for the buildings and pay the pastor.

The state has been wrong to take over this responsibility. The Bible says that God has given the civil government responsibility for administering justice (Romans 13:1-7). When the state moves beyond this and becomes a social welfare agency, it is going beyond what God allows and taking a responsibility that belongs to the family.

A second problem is that governments are very inefficient in providing social welfare. In many wealthy nations, the civil government is spending more than a quarter of all that is produced on social welfare, but they have not been able to get rid of poverty. Poverty has worsened as social welfare has grown.

Government funds are administered by a bureaucracy, so most of the money does not get to the poor. It goes to pay the salaries of those who administer the social welfare programmes. Their programmes tend to be impersonal, so it is impossible to distinguish between the bludgers and those with a genuine need. Worse still, government programmes tend to produce a class of people who are dependent on social welfare. They tend to perpetuate the problem, rather than solving it.

Deacons would do the job much more efficiently. They would usually be unpaid volunteers, so all the money would go to those who are in need. They would have personal contact with those that they are helping, so they could quickly weed out those who were bludging. The money would go to those with genuine needs. Most important of all, they would teach those who are poor to manage without help. This would mean that monetary help would always be given on a short-term basis.

Sometimes the help will be given as a loan. Interest-free loans are a key form of Christian charity (Deut 15:1-11). They maintain the person's self esteem, while providing an incentive for them to get back onto their feet.

A third problem with government social welfare schemes is the effect that they have on family life. God has given fathers the responsibility for providing for their families and where the father or his family fails to provide, the church is responsible to meet the need. When the state becomes the provider, it takes this responsibility away from the father and he loses his self respect. This weakens family life, making the whole welfare problem worse.

The worst effect of government social welfare is the effect that it has on the incentive to work and succeed. People no longer have to work to supply their needs, because the government will provide for them. Those who do work are taxed heavily, to pay the cost of social welfare. They soon get the feeling that it does not pay to work hard and the whole economy is weakened.

In many countries, more and more people are depending on benefits from the welfare state, while fewer and fewer people are working to support it. The whole system is already strained, and will eventually collapse. This disaster will provide an opportunity for deacons to take a leading role in the reformation

> *As Christians get serious about sharing their possessions, a simple lifestyle will start to emerge.*

of society. Once the state can no longer provide for the poor, the Church will need to take up its proper responsibility. This will be a tremendous opportunity. There will be many people in need. Deacons should be getting ready, so that they can meet that need and share the gospel at the same time.

Simple Lifestyle — As Churches get serious about sharing their possessions, a simple lifestyle should start to emerge. People will still own property and possessions, but their attitudes should be very different. They will choose a simpler lifestyle, not because possessions are evil, but because they are irrelevant. Christians should be so focussed on what God is doing that they lose interest in the things that occupy the world.

If the Holy Spirit is really moving in power, Christians will find it hard to be absorbed in a newer house or a bigger yacht? If the Lord is "adding to their number daily", "retail therapy" will seem quite boring. If there is great joy in their neighbourhood, because paralytics and cripples are being restored, who would be dreaming about upgrading their car? The members of a Church will be so involved in the work of the Holy Spirit, that they will lose the need to own more and more things.

Sharing will mean that Christians can live better than the rest of society, while owning fewer possessions. Consequently, they will be able to spend less time working for money and more time working for the Lord. If they are called to work, they will be able to give more freely to support people in need. Sharing will free up resources for the work of the Kingdom. If God's people learn to live simply and to share what they have, deacons will be able to use the surplus to minister to people in need.

South American Analogy — Roberto lives in a favela (shantytown) on a hill above a large South American city. The church cannot meet in his house because it is too small. It meets under a tree beside the track that goes past his house. The meetings are not private and everyone can see what is happening, but that is the way life is in the favelas.

The church was started by Rodrigo and Eduado, who were sent into the favela from a Church based in a better part of the city. They met Roberto when he was begging for money to pay for his wife's medical care. She was dying of tuberculosis. They did not give him money, but offered to go to his home and pray for her. She was dramatically healed, so she and Roberto gave their lives to the Lord. They invited Rodrigo and Eduado to stay in their home and start a church. Although they were elders in their home church, others were able to take over from them and support their vision for the favela.

This was six months ago and now a group of about twenty Christians are meeting regularly under the tree outside their home. Rodrigo is already teaching Roberto how to disciple some of them. For Rodrigo and Eduado living in the favela was a real culture shock, but they stuck to it, because they could see the Holy Spirit at work.

CHAPTER TEN

The Apostle

Jesus gave some to be apostles, so the body can expand

When a Church reaches an optimum size some of the elders will be sent out to start a new Church. The pastor-teachers sent out are called apostles. Sometimes the prophet accompanying them is also called an apostle.

This is what happened in the church in Antioch (Acts 13:1-3). In that church there were prophets and teachers (pastors). While they were at prayer, the Holy Spirit told them to set aside Paul and Barnabas to be apostles.

Paul and Barnabas then went through Asia Minor establishing new churches. This is the ministry of the apostle. Once Paul and Barnabas had been sent out, Luke always called them apostles (Acts 14:14).

An apostle is an elder who is sent out to establish a new church. The Greek word "apostlos" literally means one who is sent. It is applied to a messenger who is sent on a mission. In the New Testament, it is used to describe a person who is sent out to establish a new Church.

When starting a new Church, apostles will normally move into the next neighbourhood or village. Often they will go to a place where someone has just been converted (Acts 16:11-15). They will go where the Spirit is moving, so hearing God's voice will be important in knowing where to go.

In warfare, establishing a new beachhead is much harder than pushing out from controlled territory. The same applies in the spiritual dimension. New ministries often go and try to establish a base in the toughest part of the city with very little close support. Success in these situations requires a great deal of intercession and spiritual warfare. Advancing from an area where a spiritual stronghold has been established will be less demanding and more likely to be successful.

Send the Best — The best people should be sent out. Paul and Barnabas were key leaders in the church at Antioch, so they were sent out as apostles. This is a most important principle. Most new works fail, because the best leader stays behind and an inexperienced person is sent out to start something new. Starting a new Church is harder than keeping a good Church going, so the best people should be assigned to this task.

> *The best elders should be sent out as apostles.*

In the early days of the church the apostles all stayed in Jerusalem. This may have been nice for them, but it held back the growth of the church. God had to send persecution to get them to move out into the world. It was among those who fled to Antioch that the next major advance of the church took place (Acts 8:1-8; 11:19-21). The Lord may have to send a time of testing in the modern church to get those who are called to be apostles to move out.

Being sent out as an apostle will be quite humbling. The apostle will be going from something that is growing and strong to a new work that is tiny. Sending the best may seem like a waste of skills, but the best people are needed in the new Church.

Send Teams — Apostles should never be sent out alone. Even a mature Christian like Paul took others with him for support and spiritual protection. Sending a person or couple out alone to start a new Church is like sending soldiers armed with sticks to fight against tanks. We should not be surprised that so many are destroyed in these circumstances.

The members of the apostolic team must have developed strong relationships with each other by working together in the Church from which they are sent. The elders being sent out as apostles will need to function as the elders of the new Church. They will submit to each other in the same way as elders of any other Church. This will provide protection from sin and the attacks of Satan. If they have not proved they can work together in the sending Church, they should not be expected to work together in a new environment.

Balanced Teams — The apostolic team should be a balanced team. An apostle must always be accompanied by a prophet. Barnabas (Acts 4:36) and Silas (Acts 15:32) were prophets who accompanied Paul. When Paul and Barnabas had a disagreement, Paul was not prepared to go out till he had found another prophet (Silas) to go with him.

The most experienced prophet should be sent out with the apostle, because starting the new Church is the most demanding task. Good prophetic insight must be part of the Church from the beginning, so it will be built on a foundation of righteousness and holiness. Every new work must be based on a clear vision. Many new works founder, because they have inadequate or confused vision.

The apostle and the prophet complement each other. This is why a Church is said to be "built on the foundation of apostles and prophets" (Eph 2:20). The apostle will use his pastoral experience to draw a group of believers together and build them into a unit. The prophet will impart vision and zeal into the new Church. He will give encouragement to the apostle and watch over the Church to see that it is built according to God's plan. A building with a faulty foundation will not be able to stand, and will eventually collapse.

The apostolic team should also include an evangelist. Timothy (2 Tim 4:5) and Mark (he wrote a gospel) were evangelists who accompanied Paul. The evangelist would have specific responsibility for sharing the gospel.

In this diagram, the pastor (S) has been sent out and becomes an apostle (A). A prophet (P) and evangelist (E) were sent out with him.

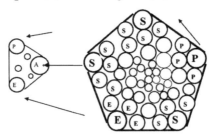

Before leaving, the apostles will appoint new elders to take over their responsibilities in the sending Church. The new elders will step up easily, because they have learned their ministries, while being supervised by the departing elders. Replication of ministries is an essential part of this process. If the new elders have been trained by their predecessors, the sending Church will carry on with very little disruption.

The new Church will grow quickly. The evangelist in the team will ensure there are plenty of new converts. Having a very experienced pastor-teacher will ensure they grow quickly. The apostle will train some of the new converts to be pastor-teachers. Once the new Church has grown a little, the more mature of the new converts will be appointed as elders.

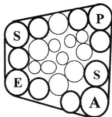

The New Testament Way — Jesus gave very clear instructions about the way that an apostolic team should do its work (Luke 10). When they are sent out into a new area, they should seek God to find the right neighbourhood.

*After this the Lord appointed seventy-two others and sent them two
by two ahead of him to every town and place where he was about
to go (Luke 10:1).*

Jesus appointed the seventy-two and sent (literally apostled) them
out. They went everywhere he was going to go. Now that Jesus
has gone and the Holy Spirit has come, apostles should go where
the Holy Spirit is about to go. Being in Jerusalem is pointless, if
the Holy Spirit is moving in Antioch.

Some neighbourhoods and nations are spiritually tougher than
others. Jesus said,

*When you enter a town and are not welcomed, go into its streets
and say, 'Even the dust of your town that sticks to our feet we wipe
off against you. Yet be sure of this: The kingdom of God is near'
(Luke 10:10,11).*

Apostles should not waste their efforts where they are not welcome.
They should move on and find a place where the Holy Spirit is
moving. Antioch is a good example of such a place, but the apostles
initially missed out on the opportunity (Acts 11:20-24).

Person of Peace — When they move to the chosen location, the
apostles should try to establish contact with an influential person
or "person of peace" in that place. Jesus commanded the seventy-
two to stay in one home and not go from house to house.

*When you enter a house, first say, 'Peace to this house.' If a man of
peace is there, your peace will rest on him; if not, it will return to
you (Luke 10:5,6).*

He had said something very similar when he sent out the twelve.

*Whatever town or village you enter, search for some worthy person
there and stay at his house until you leave. As you enter the home,
give it your greeting. If the home is deserving, let your peace rest on it;
if it is not, let your peace return to you (Matt 10:11-13).*

The Holy Spirit will lead the apostles to a "worthy person" or
"person of peace". This is someone who is open to the gospel
and who has contact and influence with other people in the area.
Sometimes that person might be a Christian with a burden for

their neighbourhood. The new Church will usually meet in the house of the person of peace.

Paul often went to the local synagogue to identify the worthy person. This was how he and Barnabas started a Church in the house of Lydia.

> One of those listening was a woman named Lydia, a dealer in purple cloth from the city of Thyatira, who was a worshiper of God. The Lord opened her heart to respond to Paul's message. When she and the members of her household were baptised, she invited us to her home. "If you consider me a believer in the Lord," she said, "come and stay at my house." And she persuaded us (Acts 16:14,15).

Lydia was the person of peace and influence and the first convert in Philippi. Paul and Barnabas established a church in her house.

The Person of Peace will have influence in their neighbourhood and potential to become an elder.

Sometimes the person of peace or influence will be a town official or key business person. Publius, the chief official of Malta welcomed Paul into his home (Acts 28:7). Lydia was a successful businesswoman. In Paphos, the proconsul, Sergius Paulus, sent for Barnabas and Saul because he wanted to hear the word of God (Acts 13:6,7). Winning a person in authority for Christ will open the whole neighbourhood or village up to the gospel.

The fact that the person is at peace may be a sign that the forces of evil are not strong in that locality. This will make it an ideal place to establish a spiritual stronghold.

Stay in a House — In most cultures, the apostles would go and live in the house of the person of peace. Jesus said,

> Stay in that house, eating and drinking whatever they give you, for the worker deserves his wages. Do not move around from house to house. (Luke 10:7).

Jesus had said the same thing to the twelve when he sent them out.

> Whatever house you enter, stay there until you leave that town (Luke 9:4).

Paul and Barnabas went to stay with Lydia. Paul went to stay with Publius. Ideally an apostolic team would accept customary offers of hospitality and stay in the house of the person of peace.

In western cultures, staying with the person of peace or influence might be too intrusive. The apostle should rent or buy a house as close as possible to the person of influence, but they would still have their meetings in the home of the person of peace.

If the rest of the apostolic team are single, they could stay with the apostle in his house. If they are married, they should find houses close by.

The apostolic team will focus on their chosen locality. They will build a spiritual stronghold and form a Christian community, in which they share and care for each other. This will be a tremendous witness to the people who live around them.

Healing the Sick — Once contact has been established with the person of peace, the apostles should look for opportunities to heal the sick. Jesus said,

> When you enter a town and are welcomed, eat what is set before you. Heal the sick who are there and tell them, 'The kingdom of God is near you' (Luke 10:8,9).

An apostle has authority to heal the sick, so someone should be healed, when the apostolic team moves into the new neighbourhood. The healing will often crack the neighbourhood open.

At Malta, Paul prayed for Publius's sick father and he was healed (Acts 28:8-10). The whole island came and were healed (many would have been saved). The proconsul in Paphos believed the Gospel, when he saw a sorcerer struck blind by the Holy Spirit (Acts 13:8-12).

When people in the neighbourhood hear about the healing, they will be curious. Many others will come wanting to be healed. The apostles will take the opportunity to share the gospel and pray for them.

In most cultures, a crowd will gather. The apostle or the evangelist will preach the gospel and pray for the sick. God will confirm their preaching with signs and wonders (Mark 16:20). Jesus regularly used this method.

The apostolic team will disciple the new Christians, teaching them to live in obedience to Jesus. They will mould them together into a Church, based in the home of the person of peace. The new Church will become a community in which the life of Christ is visibly demonstrated. As households are converted, they will be drawn into this community. Seen from this perspective, becoming a Christian is becoming part of a Christian community.

Starting with the End in Mind — Apostles will start the new Church with the end in mind. The first priority of the apostolic team will be to get to the stage where they can appoint a team of elders from within the new Church to take over its leadership. Most of their energy will go into those whom they expect to become elders. The apostolic team will intensively disciple them and start to replicate their ministries in them. They will focus on developing a team containing the full range of ministries.

People with influence are important because they are likely to become leaders in the new Church. A person of peace is less likely to have a lot of personal problems that need to be sorted out before they can grow into leadership. A person with both influence and a peaceful spirit should have potential to become an elder.

The ideal is for the apostle to live with the person of peace. This would increase the intensity of their discipleship. They would see everything the apostle does and be able to join in all the apostle's activities. Having an apostle, and perhaps a prophet, living in their house will also provide a high level of spiritual protection. These benefits will help the person of peace grow very fast.

The apostolic team will not be concerned about gathering a large number of new converts. They will be busy with those who have leadership potential, so they will not have time to disciple a large number of new converts. They will not want a lot of new converts until some of the first batch of local Christians is ready to disciple them.

A work is 'unfinished" until local elders have been appointed (Tit 1:5). When a local eldership team is in place, it will be easier to bring people into the Church.

Apostles will not be interested in church buildings. Their focus will be on growing to the point where they are able to send out apostles again, so they will not waste time and resources on buildings. Sending out apostles and starting new Churches is more important than a place to meet. The members of the apostolic team will usually rent their houses, as they will want to be free to move on when the time is right.

The New Testament Way
- Go where the Holy Spirit is moving
- Seek the person of peace
- Get established in a house
- Heal the sick
- Preach the gospel
- Make disciples
- Establish a Church
- Train elders
- Go out again

Effective Strategy — Jesus spelt out a very clear strategy, but implementing it will require a radical change in the mindset of the church. For a long time the goal has been to get people to come to the church to hear the gospel. The problem with this approach is that in many cultures, most non-Christians will not come into a church service.

Jesus never said we should get people to come; he always said the church should go to where the people are (Matt 28:19; Mark 16:15; Luke 24:47; Acts 1:8). The advantage of the New Testament way outlined here is that the Church goes to where the people live. They will see real hard-core Christianity being lived out in their living room or in the house next door.

The Path of an Apostle — An apostle does not rest on his laurels. Once a new Church has grown to the point where local elders can be appointed, the apostolic team will be sent out a second time. The path of an apostle can be described by the following diagram. Each little pentagon signifies a Church with a balanced ministry.

 The Church that sent out the original apostolic team is signified by the shading. In this example the first Church has sent an apostle who has started a new Church.

Once the new Church reaches maturity, new elders are appointed and the apostolic team moves out again to start another Church. The apostle replicates his ministry and then moves on to repeat the process. The arrowheads represent new Churches.

The first Church has also trained up some new elders and sent out another apostolic team. (The best and most experienced will be sent out).

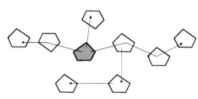 Several years later the original apostle has started a third Church. The first Church he planted has sent out another apostolic team. The original Church has now sent out three apostolic teams.

A few years later, 6 new Churches have been started as apostles have been commissioned and sent out. In each case, the best people have been sent.

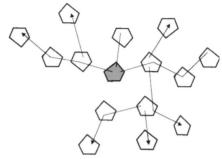

A few years later there are twenty-five Churches. Multiplication is a very powerful principle as it produced exponential growth.

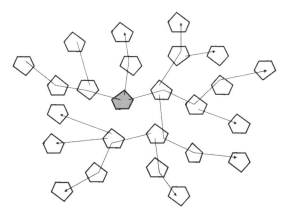

Biological Growth — The whole church will grow in the same way as a body grows. As each cell grows, a small nucleus will split off to form a new cell, resulting in two cells in the place of one.

In this way a whole city could be won for Christ; not by drawing people into a large central church, but by increasing the number of Churches. As one neighbourhood or street is won for the Lord, a new Church could be started in the next neighbourhood. Gradually as the number of Churches expands the whole city will be won. There will be a Church in every neighbourhood of the city.

In a city where the people live in apartments, Churches will look different, but the process will be the same. The aim will be to have several churches in each apartment block. Apostolic teams will often just be sent to the next apartment building to establish a new Church. Rural areas will be won in the same way, as apostles go from village to village establishing churches.

Churches should not multiply by dividing in half, as is sometimes suggested. Most Christians hate this because it breaks relationships that they have put effort into building. Under the apostolic model described here, most of the people in the sending Church can continue as normal. They will already have good relationships with the new elders, so they will be unaffected by the departure of the apostles. Their relationships with other friends in the Church can continue to grow and develop.

Those sent out will often return to their sending church for fellowship and encouragement, so the bonds will not be broken.

Overseas Mission — Some apostles will be sent out to other countries as missionaries. The best people should be given the toughest tasks, so those sent into other cultures should be very experienced apostles. Starting a Church in a strange culture is very difficult. Sending beginners out to practice is an insult to the receiving nation. If we really care about other nations, we should send out the best. The best we can offer is an apostolic team that has proved it can work together and establish effective Churches.

Apostles should never be sent into a different culture alone. Sending an individual or couple into a different culture, puts them at tremendous spiritual risk. An apostle should be sent out in a team that includes at least one pastor, one prophet and one evangelist. Otherwise the Church in the new country will be unbalanced.

An apostolic team should have established good working relationships in their own country, before they are sent out. Forming a missionary team with members of different churches and different countries gives them the burden of learning to work together, while coping with the pressures of a new environment.

Before they are sent out to another culture, an apostolic team should have proved their ability by planting a church in their own culture. Paul and Barnabas were only sent out after they had proved themselves in Antioch. Sending teams that have never planted a church to work in a mission field is very optimistic. They will have to learn how to build a church while coping with the pressure of a hostile environment. We should not be surprised if they struggle to get things off the ground.

An apostolic team sent to another country should concentrate on establishing a Church in a particular locality. Once they have trained up elders to take over, they should start the process of multiplication by being sent out to start another Church in a new area. At some stage, they will take indigenous Christians with them to teach them how to be apostles. Very soon some of the indigenous Christians should also be sent out as apostles, so the indigenous Church can multiply independently.

The Pillars of the Church — Apostles are the pillars of the Church (Galatians 2:9). In the diagram, the apostles represented by the dots have all started at least two new Churches and some have started three. The first apostle (large dot) has planted four.

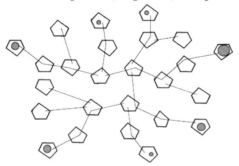

The important thing to note is that the best people are at the outside. However, the seven dots are not just seven individuals. Each dot represents an apostolic team, so there are at least twenty top people at the cutting edge. Their broad range of experience and variety of ministries will provide real protection and strength for the Church as a whole. The strongest Christians are on the battlefront with the world, where the spiritual battle is toughest. Apostles are the pillars of the church, because they are on the edge of the church holding it up.

Apostolic Authority — Apostles will have an important role in maintaining order in the Churches. They will deal with problems that could harm a Church. However, apostles exercise authority by "looking back". This is important.

The first apostle is represented in the diagram by a large dot. Elders in each of the shaded Churches have a link with him. They will be either his spiritual children or spiritual grand children, so they will respect him and acknowledge his authority. Often they submitted to him when he was an elder and they were new Christians. They will still respect him, though they have become elders. Most of the other Churches will have a similar relationship with the apostle represented by the smaller dot. These two apostles will be respected and given spiritual authority in most of the Churches in the diagram.

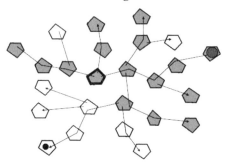

The authority of an apostle comes out of relationship. Paul demonstrated this type of authority in his letters. He gave direction to the leaders of the churches. He suggested solutions to problems that had surfaced. His authority was important for keeping the churches functioning correctly. Paul was able to give direction to these churches because he had a relationship with them. He was one of the apostles who had established their church.

When Paul was unable to make personal contact with the elders in a church (because he was in prison), he would send a colleague, who knew his heart to work on his behalf. For example, Timothy was sent to Ephesus (1 Tim 1:3) and Titus was sent to Crete (Titus 1:5). These men had credibility in these Churches, because they had a good relationship with Paul.

Spiritual authority comes out of relationship. The authority of an apostle is a moral authority, completely different from the authority of a bishop or an executive in the worldly pyramid model. It does not depend on legal authority or appointment to a position, but on relationships of trust and influence.

A few Churches will disobey God, reject their apostles and grieve the Holy Spirit. Authority based on relationship cannot be enforced. If the elders

> *Apostles exercise authority by "looking back" to the people who sent them out.*

in a Church lose the plot and refuse to acknowledge the authority of the other apostles, they will be powerless.

Most large churches lose a significant number of people every year and many of these never come back to the Lord. When the pastor/leader goes off the rails, many more are hurt or lost. The good thing about the structure described in this book is that a Church that grieves the Holy Spirit will quickly die, because it does not have institutional support to sustain it. While this is sad, only a small number of people will be hurt. Most will just walk away.

Apostles and Unity — The body of Christ will be made up of an extremely large number of small Churches. And just as individual members of a local Church have different gifts and ministries, each Church will have a different function. Each Church will specialise in a particular type of ministry. This specialisation will increase the effectiveness of the whole Church.

In the created world there is infinite variety. God will create a similar variety within the body of Christ. The calling of a Church will arise out of the dreams, giftings and ministries of its members, so no two Churches will exercise exactly the same function. The whole body will be made complete, as each Church fulfils its calling and complements the others.

Within this diversity, God stills intends his Church to be united. The main source of unity will be the apostles. They will continually "look back" to the Churches they established to build unity and resolve differences between them. The apostles and elders working in a region will maintain relationships with each other. Many will have grown up in the same Churches and will know each other well.

Sometimes all the apostles and elders in an area will meet informally to encourage each other or to resolve a problem.

This is what happened when Paul visited Miletus on the way to Jerusalem (Acts 20:17). He gave his teaching and exhortation to the elders of the Churches of Ephesus. They would have taken Paul's teaching and anointing back to their own Churches.

Acts 15 describes a meeting of apostles and elders to resolve a dispute between churches over obedience to the law. This was not a church council because it had no legal authority. It was an informal meeting to settle a dispute between two Churches. The apostles took a lead because they had discipled most of the elders present, so their wisdom was respected.

The other source of unity is the Holy Spirit. Each Church will be led and directed by him, carrying out the role that he assigns to it. He will do what Jesus commands, so although there will be many Churches, Jesus will be the Lord of each Church. Unity of purpose will come through submission to The Holy Spirit.

Normal Church Life — We need a new standard for deciding when a Church is successful. A church may grow rapidly in numbers, without its members growing to maturity. A successful Church will be producing elders who can be sent out as apostles. In the church at Antioch there were prophets and teachers who could be sent out as apostles. It may not have been a large church, but it showed the sign of true maturity.

A new Church should not wait too long before sending out an apostolic team. As soon as people are ready to take over the leadership, the apostles should be sent on to start a new Church. The sooner this happens, the better. Once a Church grows beyond a certain size, its leaders become indispensable and it will be too hard to replace the elders who are sent out. It is more likely to get institutionalised. An established Church is much harder to mobilise than a new one.

A Church that is continually sending out apostles will be an exciting place to be. There will be no room for complacency to creep in. If a Church is continually sending out apostles there will always be a challenge for the remaining members. They will have an opportunity to grow into leadership. Potential leaders will be constantly stepping up into the roles of those who have left. This will be a tough challenge for them, but they will not get bored. When people get bored and restless, problems follow.

The pastor/leader says it is tough at the centre and harder than being sent out. He is correct, but his task is hard because he is often surrounded by bored, purposeless, proud, critical or lazy Christians. His church is often full of people who have remained as spiritual infants, because the structure of the church did not allow them to grow into eldership ministries.

No Superstars — Most elders can become apostles. In fact, many of the apostles in the New Testament were such ordinary people (Barnabas, Andronicus, Junias), that we know very little about them. They were not super apostles. If we were to stop looking for the spectacular, we would find there are many people in our churches who are called to be apostles.

The Greek word for apostle is used frequently in the New Testament. The problem for us is that the noun is translated "apostle", but the verb is translated as "sent". When we see the word "sent" in the New Testament, we should think "apostle". We would then realise that being "apostled" was not limited to a few "big names", but was very common.

Sending out apostles is something that every church should be doing. They may not be in the same league as Paul or Silas, but they could exercise valid ministries, if they were recognised

> *A successful Church will be producing elders who can be sent out as apostles.*

and released. If there is rapid growth in the number of Churches, there will always be an opportunity for people to exercise this ministry.

Not every pastor will become an apostle. Some will prefer to stay where they are and work with those who are crushed and broken. That is just as valid a ministry as being sent out as an apostle. Balanced Churches need both ministries.

Marks of an Apostle

1. Pastoral and teaching experience in a Church is essential. An apostle must have proved that they have the ability to build a Church, by discipling young Christians and by building strong relationships between believers.
2. An apostle must have the ability to proclaim the gospel. Paul was a very effective preacher of the gospel. An apostle needs the skills of both the pastor and the evangelist.
3. The ministry of the apostle is confirmed by signs and wonders (2 Cor 12:12). God immediately confirmed Paul's ministry as an apostle in Paphos, when he struck a sorcerer blind (Acts 13:6-12). An apostle should have demonstrated the gift of miracles necessary for operation of the New Testament Way.
4. Apostles should have some practical skills by which they can earn their support. Paul often supported himself as a tentmaker.
5. A person with an apostolic calling will have a holy restlessness. They may move house and change jobs frequently. They will get dissatisfied with long-term routine and will seek tough new challenges. Paul had an ambition to take the gospel where it had not been heard (Rom 15:20).
6. Apostles should not have too many dependants, so they are free to move from place. This is why Paul said it was better for some people to remain single (1 Cor 7:29-35). He was not establishing a principle of celibacy, but recognising that being single gave him tremendous freedom to follow the calling of God. Married apostles can work just as effectively, if they are equally committed.
7. An apostle must be sent, so a leader is not entitled to the name apostle until they have been sent out to replicate their work. That is the basic meaning of the word. Many church leaders are calling themselves apostles because they have successfully established a ministry or have a group of leaders who relate to them. They may be undertaking some aspects of the apostolic calling, but they are not apostles. The essence of the apostolic is being "sent out", so a person who stays at headquarters cannot be an apostle.

The Twelve Apostles — Acts 1:13 is not just a list of apostles. The use of the word "and" follows a pattern which links various apostles together.

> When they arrived, they went upstairs to the room where they were staying. Those present were Peter, John, James and Andrew; Philip and Thomas, Bartholomew and Matthew; James son of Alphaeus and Simon the Zealot, and Judas son of James (Acts 1:13).

The passage describes five apostolic teams. Each team was balanced, having one person with pastoral skills and another with a prophetic gifting. The teams were:

- Peter, John, James and Andrew. (They seem to have been the Jerusalem team. Peter was probably the prophetic one).
- Philip and Thomas (Thomas was the prophetic one because he liked to see things in black and white (John 20:24-29)).
- Bartholomew and Matthew.
- James the son of Alpheus and Simon the Zealot (the latter was zealous, so probably prophetic).
- Judas the son of James had no partner because Judas Iscariot had dropped out. (Judas Iscariot challenged Jesus, so he was probably prophetic. Here is a warning for prophets. Jesus may have been betrayed by a prophetic person).

These men had already proved that they could work together in pairs (Mark 6:7,12,13).

The apostles cast lots to choose a replacement and partner for Judas the son of James (Acts 1:21-26). Matthias was selected. Many commentators say that the eleven got this wrong, because Matthias was not heard of again. They suggest that Paul was the one God chose to be the twelfth Apostle. This understanding is incorrect. The twelve were not a select group, with a special role; they were just the first of many apostles sent out to establish churches. Matthias was chosen, not to maintain the size of the club, but as an apostolic partner for Judas the son of James.

The reason that Matthias was not heard of again was that he obeyed Jesus command to take the gospel to the nations (Acts 1:8). While the first team stayed in Jerusalem area, the other four teams took the gospel to the four corners of the earth. According to tradition Thomas died in India. The book of Acts records the growth of the church in Asia Minor, but that is only part of the story of the early church. We tend to forget that Col 1:6 reports that the gospel was bearing fruit all over the world. This was the work of the forgotten apostles. Their deeds are not written in the scriptures, but they are recorded in heaven.

Financial Support — For this model of church growth to work, Churches will need to go back to meeting in believer's homes. This will keep the overhead costs involved in planting a new Church very low. All that will be needed is a team of apostles and a home in which to meet. Often that home will be that of the first person converted, so there will be almost no expenses.

Sometimes the sending Church will support the apostles financially. The sending Church will at least support them in prayer. Paul received financial support from the Philippians, while he was in Macedonia and Thessalonica (Phil 4:14,16). At other times he supported himself by working as a tent maker. Some apostles will support themselves by working part time.

African Adventure — Katele Siloka and Samuel Chaamba lived in a very small African village called Bfwane. They were two of five elders in a Church that met under a large tree on the edge of the village. The Church had about forty members and included most of the village. It had been established by two young men from Australia who had lived in the village for two years. They had left about a year ago to start a new Church in the south of the country. Only a few of the villagers had chosen to reject the gospel.

Katele was a big soft-hearted man, loved by everyone in the village. Many of the young men jokingly called him "Father". Samuel was a lot tougher, but everyone respected him. A few years ago, he had opposed a proposal from two young Americans to mine for diamonds on land near the village. The two men went on to another village, but their venture failed and the village people were left with some large debts. The people of Bfwane were glad of Samuel's warning. Both Katele and Samuel had been discipled by the young men from Australia.

Several of the Christians in the village had been following Jesus for some time and were ready for an eldership role. They were already doing most of the discipling of any new Christians. The elders had been praying about the village of Notengane, where the old religion was still practised openly. It had a reputation for being hostile to the gospel. They had already agreed to send Katele and Samuel to the village as apostles and had been engaging in spiritual warfare to prepare for that event.

The elders had already agreed that Kalusha and Chella would take over from Katele and Samuel when they left. They did not have to make a decision, because everyone in the village could see that they were going to step up to be elders. Kalusha was kind and loving like Katele. Chella had been following Samuel around since he became a Christian and even spoke in definite tones like him.

When Katele and Samuel set out for Notengane they took Thabo with them. He was a young man who loved to preach the gospel. He had been nagging about going to Notengane almost as long as he had been a Christian.

The 15 kilometre journey to Notengane took most of the day, but their hearts were excited as the walked along the dusty road carrying heavy packs. When they arrived at their destination, it was already evening and people were busy preparing their evening meal. They were met by a young child walking with a rough crutch cut from a tree. The girl's left leg was withered and dragged behind her as she hobbled along. When they saw her, Katele and Samuel both sensed the Holy Sprit stirring in their hearts. She stood gazing at them with a look of curiosity on her face. Katele grinned and said, "Look at me". As she stared intently at them, Samuel said, "Be healed in Jesus name!" As he spoke the Holy Spirit began to flow into her leg and within a few minutes her leg was restored to full strength.

The young girl began to shriek and yell. She threw her crutch into the air and began to run towards her house. People heard the noise and came out of their houses to see what was happening. Soon a crowd gathered around and there was an amazing commotion. Everyone was talking and asking how it had happened. Her parents were both weeping. She kept pointing to the three men standing praying at the entrance to the village.

When they noticed where she was pointing, they all rushed over to where the men were waiting quietly. "Who are you?" "What have you done?" "Did you do this?" The questions tumbled out with no one waiting for an answer. Then Thabo called out in a strong voice. "I will tell you what has happened!" and he began to preach the gospel.

Thabo had been speaking boldly for about five minutes and was just making the point that Jesus is alive and real, when the village witch doctor arrived on the scene. He pushed his way to the front of the crowd and began to threaten the three men with all kinds of curses. Samuel looked at him and spoke sharply. "You have had ten years to heal this girl and you did nothing. The true God is working here so you had better not oppose him." He spoke with such authority that the villagers cheered and the old man had no alternative but to shuffle away.

Thabo did not get to finish his sermon, but it did not really matter because the young girl was still standing beside him with a smile that wrapped right around her face. It turned out that her father Kabanda was one of the elders in the village. He invited the three men to come and eat with his family. After the meal Kabanda invited Katele and Samuel to stay in his house. He found a place for Thabo in his brother's house.

The next day, seven of the village men came to talk with the men from Bfwane. They sat in a circle and talked about the gospel for most of the day. At the end of the day, they went down to the river and five of the men were baptised. Kabanda and his wife and daughter were also baptised.

A year later, most of the people in the Notengane had become Christians. The witch doctor had died, but his wife said that he was whispering "Jesus, Jesus, Jesus", as his breath ebbed away. Katele was still staying with Kabanda and his family and he spent a lot of time with Kabanda and his brother. He had taught them most of what he knew of the gospel and they were already discipling some of the newer Christians. One of the other village men had been drawn to Samuel and had started following him around taking in everything that he said. Samuel had moved to his house, so he could teach him more.

Katele and Samuel were already praying about moving on to another village. A young man, who had lived in that village when he was young, had a passion to go back and share the gospel with his people. They had promised that they would go with him when the time was right.

CHAPTER ELEVEN

Worship

Grow up into him who is the Head

When a Church comes together for worship, every believer should come expecting to contribute something to the meeting. One person will have a prayer, some will have a hymn or a spiritual song, and another will have a word of instruction or encouragement. Others may bring messages from God through prophecy or tongues and interpretation. Most people present should make a contribution to the worship.

> *They broke bread in their homes and ate together with glad and sincere hearts, praising God and enjoying the favour of all the people (Acts 2:46,47).*
>
> *When you come together, everyone has a hymn, or a word of instruction, a revelation, a tongue or an interpretation. All of these must be done for the strengthening of the church (1 Cor 14:26).*

The Holy Spirit is the Worship Leader — The Holy Spirit will be the worship leader. The whole meeting will be led and co-ordinated by him to accomplish his purposes. He will inspire the various contributions in such a way as to give unity and order, even though they come from different people. He will prompt each believer to make his contribution at the right time. The whole Church will worship God together in the Spirit and in truth.

The elders will not lead the worship. Instead the service will begin with waiting for the Holy Spirit, so that the he can do what he wants to do. There will be no strict order of service, but the Holy Spirit will be free to do something different each time. Sometimes the emphasis will be on worship, but at other times he may concentrate on intercession, teaching, repentance, healing hurt people, restoration of relationships, or evangelism. The Holy Spirit is creative, so he will inspire an infinite variety of worship.

Allowing the Holy Spirit to lead the worship will be risky, but exhilarating

Seeing the Holy Spirit bring a coherent service together through different people will be exciting. If he does not come to the meeting, the whole Church would be embarrassed. The fear that nothing might happen should spur people to listening to him.

Being dependent on the Holy Spirit would keep the whole Church alert and at peace with each other. Disputes and offences would have to be dealt with immediately. Passive participation in worship should be impossible. The task of the elders is not to lead the worship, but to test the contribution of the believers. The Bible says,

> Do not believe every spirit, but test the spirits to see whether they are from God (1 John 4:1).

Elders with a gift of discernment will have a particular responsibility for this task. Satan will try to disrupt the worship by sending deceiving spirits. Immature Christians seeking attention may try to dominate proceedings. The elders must recognise and reject everything that is not inspired by the Holy Spirit. Their responsibility is to keep the worship pure and holy.

Meeting Place — A Church will usually meet for worship in a home of one of the believers. If this is not possible, the Church will meet in any private place available. A four-car garage with some carpet on the floor and some cushions spread around would be ideal for a fellowship meeting. A local café bar might be a good place for meetings of the Church, if the owner and some of the patrons have been converted.

If we go back to meeting in homes, Church members may have to accept a lower level of comfort than is usually expected in the western world. There may not be an armchair for every member, but if some people are willing to stand or sit on cushions on the floor, 30 to 40 people could fit into a large lounge.

In a city where the people live in apartments, Churches will meet in the home of the member with the largest living area. As the living areas are often smaller, Churches may have to be slightly smaller. On the other hand, if people are comfortable in an enclosed space, more people may be able to fit into a meeting.

In warm climates believers will often meet outside. One Church Paul started met beside a river. In many parts of the world, Churches will meet in the open spaces of a town or village. A special sanctuary is not necessary for worship.

The first covenant had an earthly sanctuary. The new covenant has a heavenly sanctuary, where Christ reigns as High Priest (Heb 9:1,11). When Christians worship in the Spirit and in truth, they draw near to him in the Spirit. They enter into his presence in the heavenly sanctuary (Revelation 4:1-10). This means that worship can take place in any situation where a few believers are gathered. Having a special worship sanctuary is wrong, as it places the Church back in the old covenant.

One Another Stuff — Church meetings will also focus on doing the "one another stuff". The New Testament only contains one command that Christians should meet together regularly.

> *Let us not give up meeting together, as some are in the habit of doing, but let us encourage one another – and all the more as you see the Day approaching (Heb 10:25).*

The reason for meeting is to encourage and build each other up. When the Church comes together it will worship Jesus, but it will also focus on doing the "one another stuff".

Church Buildings

A special building is not essential for a church to function, so owning a building should not be a high priority. Special buildings can cause a number of problems for a church.

1. Church buildings give a distorted view of the church that is an obstacle to evangelism. Many people think that a church is an old stone building with a high-pitched roof and steeple or a large auditorium.
2. Christians can fall into the trap of thinking that Jesus is only present in the church building. His presence can be real anywhere, so we do not need to go to a special place to meet with him.
3. The design of church buildings often hinders fellowship between Christians.
4. Church buildings absorb a large amount of capital, making it unproductive. Christians should invest their capital in projects that will bear fruit for the Kingdom of God.
5. Church buildings are not practical in many large cities, as land is too expensive. In the third world, most people do not have the resources to build elaborate church buildings.

Ownership of buildings should not be a high priority for a church. The most spectacular growth in history took place in the early church, which did not own any buildings.

The Lord's Supper — The Lord's Supper will be an important aspect of worship, but it should not be a ceremony. The Greek word used in the expression Lord's Supper is "deipnon" (1 Corinthians 11:20). This word describes the main meal of the day, so supper is a misleading translation for people who think of supper as a small snack. In John 12:2, the same word is used to describe a dinner given in honour of Jesus by Lazarus. A small cube of bread and a sip of wine is not a "deipnon".

The Lord's Supper should be a shared meal. Problems arose in the Corinthian church, because some people would not share their food and others could not afford to bring food.

> *It is not the Lord's Supper you eat, for as you eat, each of you goes*
> *ahead without waiting for anybody else. One remains hungry,*
> *another gets drunk. Don't you have homes to eat and drink in? Or*
> *do you despise the church of God and humiliate those who have*
> *nothing? (1 Cor 11:20-22).*

People were keeping their own food or eating as soon as they arrived at the meeting. Paul suggested that those who were too hungry to wait for the rest of the Church should eat something at home before coming. However, this passage also tells us what Paul expected at the Lord's Supper.

• The Church should come together for a meal.
• People should bring food to share.
• Those with plenty of food should provide for those with none.
• They should wait and eat the meal together.

Paul gave a warning about the importance of sharing with the body.

> *A man ought to examine himself before he eats of the bread*
> *and drinks of the cup. For anyone who eats and drinks without*
> *recognising the body of the Lord eats and drinks judgement on*
> *himself. That is why many among you are weak and sick, and a*
> *number of you have fallen asleep. But if we judged ourselves, we*
> *would not come under judgement. When we are judged by the Lord,*
> *we are being disciplined so that we will not be condemned with the*
> *world. So then, my brothers, when you come together to eat, wait for*
> *each other. If anyone is hungry, he should eat at home, so that when*
> *you meet together it may not result in judgement (1 Cor 11:28-34).*

He warns that there is so much sickness in the church because they are not discerning or recognising the body of Christ.

By taking verses 28,29 out of context, we make failure to "discern the body" into a mystical sin of failing to honour the bread and the wine. Rather, Paul is warning that they were sick, because they had failed to show honour and commitment to other Christians. They could avoid this judgement by doing practical things like waiting for each other and sharing food.

Family Meal — The apostle Paul describes the church as the "family of God" (1 Timothy 3:15). The heart of family life is the meals that the family eats together. A family that met together less than once a week would soon disintegrate. The Lord's supper should be a regular part of our life.

> They devoted themselves to the apostles' teaching and to the fellowship, to the breaking of bread and to prayer.... They broke bread in their homes and ate together with glad and sincere hearts (Acts 2:42,46).

The early church celebrated the Lord's Supper daily in their homes. If the church goes back to meeting in homes, this would become practical again. The daily breaking of bread in their homes was an expression of their covenant with each other.

The common meal will strengthen the unity of the Church. Sharing a meal is the best way to get to know other people. As the believers eat and drink together with Jesus, they will be reminded of their relationship with him. This will flow into their commitment to each other. As they share in the Lord's meal together, their relationships with each other will be strengthened. The informality of the meal will allow them to minister to each other's needs, through the power of the Spirit.

Order of Events — The sequence of events at the Last Supper is recorded in the gospels. We should follow the same pattern when we celebrate the Lords Supper.
1. Coming together (Luke 22:14).
2. Welcome (Luke 22:15).
3. Giving thanks for the cup (Luke 22:17).
4. Eating the meal together (Mark 14:18).
5. Breaking and sharing bread, while eating (Luke 22:19, Mark 14:22).
6. End the meal by sharing the cup (Luke 22:20).

Someone should give thanks for the cup at the beginning of the meal. The bread should be broken and shared during the meal. The cup should be shared to conclude the meal. These actions will make it different from other meals and keep the focus on Jesus.

As Jesus is present, there is no need to have a special minister or priest to lead the celebration. The Lord's Supper can be celebrated wherever two or three believers are gathered, because Jesus has promised to be with them. As the bread is broken, any of those present can give thanks. When the bread and the cup are shared, Church members will serve each other. The whole meal will be simple and informal, like the shared meal that Jesus had with his disciples.

No Magic — The Lord's Supper should be a celebration with Jesus as the guest of honour. A question that has troubled the church down through the ages is how he is present. Some have suggested that the bread and wine literally change into his body and blood, but this makes the Lord's Supper into a magical experience where we receive Jesus by eating special food. This is nonsense, because Jesus is seated at the right hand of God, so we can only receive him through the presence of the Holy Spirit.

Magic is doing something physical, like eating, to make something spiritual happen. Trying to receive Jesus by eating a food in a particular way is magic, so Christians should avoid it. Approaching the Lord's Supper this way, leads to an incorrect focus on the moment of eating, hoping that something mystical will happen (often it does not). Concentrating on the bread and the cup as if these had magical properties is misguided.

The Lord's Supper is made special by the Holy Spirit glorifying Jesus in the midst of his people. Instead of nibbling on symbolic tokens, we should ask the Holy Spirit to be a guest at a meal shared with our friends.

The Holy Spirit loves to be present with Christians who are committed to each other and share their food. He gets really excited when Christians come together in unconditional commitment to each other and often brings a special revelation of Jesus to those present. This is what happened at the village of Emmaus.

> *When he was at the table with them, he took bread, gave thanks, broke it and began to give it to them. Then their eyes were opened and they recognised him, and he disappeared from their sight (Luke 24:30,31).*

The Lord's Supper is a practical experience. It should not be a highly organised ritual slotted in at the end of a worship service, but a meal that the members of a Church share together. The feature that distinguishes it from other meals is the presence of Jesus through his Spirit.

Spontaneity and Participation — During Old Testament times, access to God was only possible through a priest and only those with a special gift of the Spirit could speak on behalf of God or to him. The ministry of Jesus dramatically changed this situation, by giving all Christians direct access to God.

The outpouring of the Holy Spirit at Pentecost means that every believer is anointed, so God can speak and minister through any Christian. This brought about a radical change in the nature of worship. Christian worship should be marked by spontaneity and participation.

Unfortunately, this is often not the reality. The weekly worship service has become a highly organised and controlled event, with most people sitting passively during the service. They can sing and clap during the worship, but otherwise they remain quiet.

Spiritual needs are ministered to by the pastor and senior leaders at the front of the meeting following the preaching. This ministry at the front often does not fully deal with issues. The service is very much a performance by the pastor/leader or worship leader, while most of the people watch passively.

This performer/observer divide is not conducive to the "one another stuff". Nor does it encourage active Christianity. The presence of the Holy Spirit should bring spontaneity and participation. Their absence suggests that we are not giving him the freedom that he desires and needs to accomplish his purposes.

Children in Worship — There will be no Sunday School or special children's slot during worship, as the bible gives responsibility for teaching children to their parents, especially their fathers. Teaching is to be done as part of daily life, rather than in special teaching sessions.

Teach them to your children, talking about them when you sit at home and when you walk along the road, when you lie down and when you get up (Deut 11:19).

By providing Sunday Schools, churches have robbed parents of their role. This has led parents to neglect their teaching responsibilities.

Children should take part in all the worship activities of the Church. They may not understand everything that happens, but if their parents are participating joyfully and the Holy Spirit is doing exciting things, children will also be edified. Children are quite capable of discerning the presence of the Lord, and worshipping him.

The main need of the children and young people in a Church is good relationships with adult Christians. Each child should have another adult who is an elder to them. This adult will rejoice in the child's success, sympathise with their troubles, and encourage them always.

Preaching — Preaching should not be an important part of worship. Too much preaching at believers leaves them feeling discouraged and condemned. Quiet sharing and encouragement by the elders will be more effective in producing spiritual growth. Perpetual preaching produces passive Christians, who are more easily manipulated by false prophets.

In a world where very few people could read, regular teaching by a pastor was very important. Now that most people can read this role is redundant. A weekly sermon implies that the pastor hears God better than his people. This contrasts with 1 Cor 14: 26, where everyone has a word or revelation. It discourages Christians from seeking God's word for themselves.

Preaching belongs in the world. In the New Testament, preaching was used for evangelism. The good preachers in the church should be taken out of their pulpits and sent into the world to proclaim the good news. If the Church needs a word of direction or challenge, it is more likely to come from one of the prophets, than the pastor.

Worship Communities — The new role of "worship leader" has recently emerged in the church. This ministry is not mentioned in the New Testament, because it only became necessary after the church was institutionalised. Most worship leaders are great people with an amazing capacity for worship. They are often frustrated with their church, because other people do not have the same zeal for worship. I believe that many worship leaders are actually called to be professional worshippers in a worshipping community that ministers to God day and night.

Some Churches will become full-time worship communities. 1 Chronicles 25 describes a group of people whose role was singing and prophesying with music as part of the worship in the temple. They were divided into twenty-four shifts to support a pattern of continuous worship. This role of continuous worship was continued in some of the Roman Catholic orders, but is now dying out. A life devoted to worship has become unfashionable in a world obsessed with action. However, God is worthy of continuous worship, so this ministry should be restored in our time.

Every city should have several Churches devoted to worship. They should take turns, so that God is being continuously worshipped day and night. Only hard core worshippers will have the motivation and stamina for this task, but their worship would be so inspiring that other Christians would join them from time to time. This would bring great blessing to their city.

Celebrations — From time to time, one Church will organise a large celebration for all the Churches in a city or region. They will all come together to praise and worship God. One of the prophets may bring a message that is relevant for the time.

All the believers would be encouraged and strengthened by the experience of worshipping in a larger group. They would catch the excitement that comes with being part of something big. Therefore, a celebration should be really big. There is no reason why several thousand Christians should not gather for worship, if there are facilities large enough. It would be an exhilarating experience for the believers.

Churches should not own buildings suitable for celebrations. Combined meetings would be irregular, so it would be inefficient to own buildings just for this purpose. Any public building that is available could be used, just as the Churches in Jerusalem made use of the temple (Acts 2:46).

Ideally, a celebration should be held in a public place. A large body of Christians worshipping in unity would be a powerful witness to the community. If the climate is suitable, the celebration could be held outside in a park or stadium.

The celebration should take over and fill up one of the world's most popular meeting places. The event should be so big that it will impact on the city and be impossible to ignore. The temple in Jerusalem was the headquarters of the enemies of the early church. By filling up the temple with Christians praising God, they were really "taking it" to their opposition.

Celebrations are great, but they are not essential. The main emphasis should always be on the meetings of the individual Churches. Churches would survive even if combined meetings were not possible. If persecution were severe, it may not be possible to have a celebration, but this would not stop the church from growing. The Christians in Jerusalem met as a combined group in the temple to receive the apostles teaching, but the main fellowships were always those that met in the believer's homes (Acts 2:42-47). The time came when they were unable to meet in the temple, but the church continued growing. The persecuted church in China has also demonstrated that rapid growth is possible, even if public meetings are prohibited.

Most people attending a celebration, will be passive participants. This will not matter, if people are active in their own Churches. They will be refreshed by the anointed worship and blessed by those leading the meeting.

Celebrations should not take place too often. Where people participate in large worship groups all the time, they become apathetic. They get the feeling that plenty will happen, when they are doing nothing.

Majoring on the Minor — In the last twenty years we have seen an enormous emphasis on worship. The high point for most modern Christians is the Sunday worship service. In fact, we now talk about church as something that we go to. The worship leaders and musicians put considerable effort into preparing for it. The pastor spends even more time preparing a message for the people. Expensive sound equipment and data projection equipment is needed.

Christians usually judge the state of a church by the quality of the worship and whether they can "feel" the presence of God. The key goals for many church leaders are quality worship and preaching.

I believe that we have got this out of perspective. The problem is that we have tried to make every church meeting into a "celebration". Worship is good, but we must not forget that meeting for a celebration service is optional. Participating in a weekly celebration service can be marvellous, but it is not essential. "Feeling" the presence of God does not necessarily make us better Christians.

> *Discipling new Christians and doing the "one another stuff" are more important than worship.*

Therefore we should not be surprised (although it seems like a heresy) that the New Testament does not give the same priority to worship. Jesus did not command Christians to meet for a weekly worship service, as this would be an impossible command for many Christians. Nor does the New Testament state that we need to listen to a sermon every week. By focussing so much effort and energy on the Sunday worship celebrations, we are "majoring on the minor". We are putting our energy into something that is good, but not essential.

Discipling new Christians, building relationships and doing the "one another stuff" are more important. When they are not done, the church is severely weakened. The sad thing is that the western church is often so busy with worship that these essentials have often been squeezed out. The problem is that celebrations focus on relating to God, rather than relating to people. People can worship without having any contact with the people sitting around them, except for passing the offering bag.

Living Worship — Congregational worship is important, but our worship should not be concentrated on a couple of hours on a Sunday. All life should be an act of worship. When we submit to the will of God, our whole life becomes an act of spiritual worship, which is pleasing to God (Rom 12:1,2). Part of submitting to his will is doing the "one another stuff".

God's people should desire to worship him, but we have got the balance wrong. We put most of our energy into celebration and worship. In contrast, the New Testament states that the "one another stuff" should be the primary focus of every meeting.

Warning — Recently I attended a large worship service. A team of a dozen musicians led the worship in a very polished manner. The singing was enthusiastic and the presence of God could be felt. As we were singing a song about Jesus seated on the throne in heaven, the Holy Spirit allowed me to hear what the evil one was saying. The voice I heard said:

Who cares; I am winning.

You can do what you like in here,

I am winning out there where it all happens.

You can sing about heaven as much as you like

I am winning in the world where it counts.

This is a disturbing thought. Most modern churches put enormous energy into worship services, but we are majoring on the minor. Participating in powerful worship services can give Christians a false of impression of what their church is achieving. It can create a feeling of victory even if the church is losing ground in the world. We should be majoring on the "one another stuff". When God's people start to do this, the powers of evil will really start to tremble.

Worship at Brown Street — On Sunday, the Church in Brown Street meets together. Their meeting place is Simon's four-car garage, as they have outgrown the lounge in John's house. Simon has put some carpet on the floor and everybody brings a cushion to sit on (most just leave their cushion there). There are a few chairs around the walls for the older people to sit on.

Some of Simon's neighbours do not realise that a Church is meeting at his place. They just assume that his parties go right on till Sunday morning. Other neighbours are talking about what is going on at Simon's house, which is good.

Most Sundays start with a time of singing accompanied by acoustic guitars. The first song is one that someone feels to share their thoughts on. Other people suggest other songs as the Spirit leads. Often someone prophesies about the character of God to give focus to the worship. Other songs follow the theme of the prophecy. Some people have an anointing for worship and are good at responding to a prophecy with songs that can lift the worship.

Sometime during the singing, someone will get up and go and share a word of encouragement with someone else. They might also pray for them. The rest of the Church just carries on as if this were normal. There is usually opportunity for people to share revelations they have received, if they are relevant to the whole Church.

The meeting just flows as the Spirit leads. The elders sit among the people and only have to intervene when someone loses the plot. They don't make a fuss. They move the meeting on so quietly that most of the members do not even notice that they have intervened.

If God has a new direction for the Church, or a challenge that the elders feel the Church needs to hear, Barney or one of the others speaks for a while, but preaching is fairly rare. Generally there is time for prayer. Sometimes the whole Church prays together, but other times they break up into groups to share and pray for each other.

The meeting ends with a shared meal. Each family brings some sandwiches to share with the Church. This keeps the meal simple. The meal starts with someone breaking bread and passing it around. At the end of the meal they share a cup. This keeps the meal focussed on Jesus and God's purpose. During and after the meal there is a buzz of conversation as people share together.

Each Sunday is different. Sometimes an elder from another Church attends to share something from his heart about the city. Other times there is a focus on healing. Sometimes the whole time is taken up with worship. Often someone will bring a word of knowledge that sets the direction of the meeting. The focus is always on hearing the Holy Spirit and doing what he wants to do.

Last Sunday Mike brought a powerful prophetic word about a spirit of pride that had been creeping into the Church. It was followed by a long silence, but when one person confessed their pride to the Lord, a number of people started to weep. After Jim shared briefly about the importance of humility and the dangers of pride, a number of people openly confessed to a wrong attitude. The service ended with a sombre but joyful time of rejoicing.

This type of meeting is risky. They have had some real shambles. This does not seem to matter, as the Lord can use a shambles for good, even if just to keep them humble.

One Sunday, nothing happened for 35 minutes. Everyone sat waiting for the Holy Spirit to come but he didn't show. Finally, Barney said, "The Holy Spirit is not here, so it is a waste of time us being here. Go to your homes and see if you can find where he has gone. Come back at lunchtime and tell us what he is doing". Once everything was sorted out, there was a great rejoicing in the Lord, but lunch was quite late.

Generally, the Church strives to let the Holy Spirit do what he wants to do. They really hate getting into a rut and repeating what happened last week. Sometimes Barney has to say, "I think we are in a rut, guys. Let's pause and see what the Holy Spirit is doing".

CHAPTER TWELVE

The Kingdom of God

There is one Lord, who is over all

The Kingdom of God is the goal of history, so every Church must have a Kingdom focus. Our task is not complete when the gospel has been preached to the nations. Our commission is the Kingdom of God (Matt 28:18-20) and the Church is just a means to that end.

Jesus main purpose in coming to earth was to establish the Kingdom of God. This was the basic message that he proclaimed:

> *The time has come... The Kingdom of God is near. Repent and believe the good news (Mark 1:15).*

The gospels tell us that Jesus was constantly teaching about the Kingdom of God. The good news that he proclaimed was the gospel of the Kingdom. The twelve disciples were also sent out to proclaim the same message (Luke 9:1,2). In contrast the gospels only mention the word "church" twice.

The Kingdom includes every area of life that is under the rule and authority of God. If God rules a home it is part of the Kingdom. Where a business is run on biblical principles, it is also part of the Kingdom. The Kingdom of God includes every human activity that is done according to his will.

God intends his Kingdom to expand into every area of life. This expansion takes place in two different ways. Individual people must be born into the Kingdom. Jesus said,

Unless a man is born of water and the Spirit, he cannot enter the Kingdom of God (John 3:5).

As people are born again through repentance and faith in Jesus Christ, they become citizens of the Kingdom. God will deliver them from sickness and the power of the devil. Being born again is the only way that a person can enter the Kingdom of God.

> *The Kingdom of God is a much broader concept than the Church.*

The Kingdom also expands as Christians bring the different aspects of their lives under the authority of God. As Christians apply the principles of God's word where they have authority, those activities become part of the Kingdom of God. For example, if a husband is converted he becomes a member of the Kingdom. When he starts to run his home on biblical principles, it also becomes part of the Kingdom, since it is under the government of God. If he runs his business according to God's Word, it is also part of the Kingdom.

The Kingdom of God expands as Christians extend the rule of God into the areas of life where they have authority. This means that Christians should seek positions of authority to help the Kingdom to expand.

Authority is an essential aspect of any Kingdom. Within the Kingdom of God there are different spheres of authority. Each one involves both authority and responsibility, for those who control it. There can be no authority, without a corresponding responsibility.

God has delegated authority to various individuals and groups in society. Most spheres of authority are attached to a particular institution. When a sphere of delegated authority or institution is ruled according to his will, it becomes part of the Kingdom of God. Likewise, a church that dominates the civil government is out of order. Where authority is exercised contrary to his will, that sphere of authority is outside the Kingdom.

The interaction between the various spheres of authority must also be governed by the Word of God. One group must not take over the authority that belongs to another. For example, when the civil government becomes the provider, it is taking authority and responsibility that God has assigned to the family. Each delegated authority must only carry out the functions that God has assigned it.

Spheres of Authority and Responsibility
- The family: a husband has authority over his family. He also has a responsibility to discipline, teach, and provide for his family. His wife has a complementary responsibility and authority.
- A Business: the owner of a business has authority over his employees and other resources. He also has a responsibility to treat them according to the Word of God.
- The Church: the elders of a Church exercise authority over the members of their Church. They are responsible for the proclamation of the gospel, and the spiritual growth of their Church.
- Civil Government: The state has responsibility for the administration of justice and for the defence of the nation. It has authority to use force when carrying out these tasks.
- Personal Calling: God has given us freedom, which means that we have authority over our own lives. At the same time we are responsible to God for our behaviour.

Courts of law, schools, and voluntary societies are other important spheres of authority. Each of these institutions involves both authority and responsibility.

Full-time Ministry — The Church is just one sphere of authority within the Kingdom of God. For too long it has been seen as the only one. As a result, work in the church has been seen as the only valid form of full-time Christian service. Many people who are called to work in other areas of the Kingdom of God work full-time in the church. As this is not their true calling and they do not have the appropriate gifts, they usually become very frustrated.

The church should be releasing them to the sphere of authority where they belong. They would be working to establish the Kingdom, so they would still be involved in full-time Christian work.

Most Christians are called to a ministry outside the church in the Kingdom of God. In Israel, the Levites who looked after the temple were only about ten percent of the population. This seems to be about the right proportion. Most Christians will exercise a ministry in the Kingdom of God. Many will serve in the business world.

> *A church with an apostolic vision will train people up and send them out to work in the business world.*

The modern church has a tendency towards imperialism. Everything has to flow into it, or it is loses interest. The church always takes the best people. When a person becomes a Christian, the pastor immediately tries to find a place to use them in the church. Instead the church should send many of its better people out to work in the Kingdom of God.

A church with an apostolic vision will train people up (many useful skills can be learnt in the church), and send them out to work in the business world. For example, the church has some great musicians. The best of these should be sent out to work in the secular music industry. The direction of the flow should be reversed, so that the church is sending good people out to the business world. Elders should be training most of their disciples for ministry in the Kingdom of God.

The Church must never be an end in itself, but must always work to establish the Kingdom of God. When Jesus comes back he does not just want to find a holy Church. He is coming back for a victorious Church, a Church that has established the Kingdom of God as a reality in the world.

Kingdom Warfare — Everything outside the Kingdom of God is ruled and controlled by Satan in his kingdom of darkness. His kingdom is characterised by disunity and conflict. These are the consequences of human sin. Satan is a liar and destroyer, so his Kingdom will be full of hatred, bitterness, and destruction of human life. The only way to escape is through faith in Jesus Christ (Col 1:13).

Naturally there will be warfare between the two kingdoms. God's purpose is to extend his Kingdom throughout the entire world. Satan is also trying to expand his kingdom. His task has been made easier by Christians withdrawing from many spheres of authority. The idea has developed that politics and business are improper activities for Christians. These two very important areas of authority have been handed over to the devil. Even where Christians are involved in politics or business, there has been no serious attempt to apply biblical principles to these activities. This has severely weakened the Kingdom of God.

Instead of seeking to establish the Kingdom of God, Christians have concentrated on building the church. The church has become a place of retreat from the world. It may have supported Christians in their daily lives, but to the world it appears weak and irrelevant. Rather than being a place of retreat, the church should be a recruiting station and training ground for the Kingdom of God.

The church should recruit members for the Kingdom by proclaiming the gospel. At the same time it should send Christians out into the world to establish the Kingdom of God. Christians should move into every area of authority and take up responsibility as their Church teaches them how to exercise that authority in accordance with the Word of God.

Politics are too important to be left to the devil. Christians should get involved in politics, but they will need teaching on how to administer justice in a biblical way. They will also need strong spiritual support. Those with political authority should apply biblical principles to the government of their nation, so that it can be part of the Kingdom of God.

Churches should also be recruiting and training people to serve in business. Under modern economic conditions very few people are willing to take responsibility for employing others. This has resulted in a serious unemployment problem.

Business presents a tremendous opportunity for the expansion of the Kingdom. An employer has a great deal of influence and authority. The church should be encouraging people, who trust in God to take up this responsibility. They should begin applying biblical principles to their business, making it part of the Kingdom of God.

Freedom and the Kingdom — The Kingdom of God is a voluntary kingdom. God will never force people to obey him. The maximum force that God will ever use is the Holy Spirit working in a person's heart to draw them to himself. He wants people to choose to obey his authority. He will never force them to obey. Christians must never seize authority by force.

> *God's rule must never be established by force. We cannot build his kingdom until we win the battle in the marketplace of ideas.*

As the Holy Spirit works in the world, authority will be freely given back to God's people. If Christians are responsible, they will be appointed to positions of authority. Daniel did not have to seize authority. He was appointed to a position of authority by a king who recognised his ability (Daniel 2:46-49).

Victory of the Kingdom — As the church has retreated from the world, it has also lost its hope for the victory of the Kingdom of God. But God is in control of this universe, and he has promised that his Kingdom will be victorious. Jesus likened the Kingdom to a mustard seed that is small, but grows into a mighty tree. The Kingdom of God started off small but will grow mighty and powerful, as the rule of God spreads like leaven through the whole of society (Matthew 13:31-33).

Jesus promised that the meek would inherit the earth (Matthew 5:5). The meek are those who are submitted totally to God. As God's people submit to him, his Kingdom will spread throughout the whole earth. Because Jesus knew that God would fulfil this promise, he taught us to pray: Thy Kingdom come. He knew that the Kingdom of God would eventually come in all its fullness. There is a good picture of the glory of the Kingdom in Daniel 7:27,28.

> *Then the sovereignty, power and greatness of the kingdoms under the whole of heaven will be handed over to the saints, the people of the Most High. His kingdom will be an everlasting kingdom, and all rulers will worship and obey him.*

Daniel saw the people of God receiving the power and authority that Jesus would establish for them through his death and resurrection. He saw all those who are in places of authority submitting to God. When this happens, the Kingdom of God will have truly come.

True Hope — As the church has retreated from the world, the belief has developed that the Kingdom will not be established until Jesus returns. This is a false doctrine, that has caused Christians to sit round and wait for Jesus to come, while leaving the world in the hands of Satan.

The Bible teaches that the Kingdom of God will be established through the proclamation of the gospel, and renewed Christians applying the Word of God to every area of life. When the majority of people are Christian, and hold most positions of authority, and are exercising their authority on biblical principles, the Kingdom of God will be a reality.

The Kingdom of God is to be established by the people of God, as they proclaim the entire Word of God in the power of the Holy Spirit. Jesus Christ will be ruling his Kingdom through the Church. When the Kingdom has been established, there will be a final rebellion. Only then will Jesus return in glory, bringing the end of the world and the final judgement. The work of the Church will then be complete.

> *Then the end will come, when he hands over the kingdom to God the Father after he has destroyed all dominion, authority and power. When he has done this, then the Son himself will be made subject to him who put everything under him, so that God may be all in all (1 Corinthians 15:24,28).*

The Ambush — An ambassador was travelling to a neighbouring kingdom with a message of greeting for the king. However, he was not what he appeared to be. He had really been sent to spy out the land by his cunning and evil king, who was planning to invade the kingdom. (The good king is Jesus and the evil king is the devil.)

When the ambassador came to the border, he was surprised to find it was no longer marked. He travelled many miles down the road before he came to a border post. Those who were guarding the border had retreated far back into their kingdom.

> A weekend church
> cannot win a war.

As the ambassador travelled on the road to the king's palace, he was amazed by what he saw. The crops had been neglected and were choked by weeds. No one had bothered to harvest the grain as it ripened. It had fallen to the ground and was being eaten by the birds. In the villages, people were sick and starving. In the streets, men were fighting and killing each other. Every man was a law unto himself. In parts of the kingdom, warlords had seized control. They dominated the people who lived in their "turf", making their life a misery.

Riding into the city, the ambassador passed a statue of the good king. Children were using it for target practice and the face of the king was almost smashed to pieces. The decrees of the king had been published on a notice board, but they were covered with so much graffiti that they were unreadable.

When the ambassador came to the palace barracks, he found that most of the soldiers were drunk or asleep. The officers were squabbling among themselves about who was the greatest. They were so busy jockeying for power that they were totally unaware of what was happening in the kingdom.

The ambassador was able to walk right into the palace without being challenged. He entered the throne room where the king was surrounded by courtiers. They were all singing a song of praise to the king. When the singing stopped, a courtier cried out in a loud voice,

"We praise you O King, because you are seated on the throne!" Another courtier cried out, "We praise you O King, because your kingdom extends as far as the eye can see!" All the courtiers then gave a mighty shout and clapped and cheered their king.

The ambassador listened, thought of what he had seen, and smiled.

A king sitting on a throne cannot establish a kingdom.
He needs servants who will do his bidding,
and soldiers who will obey his commands.

As he rode back home, the ambassador noticed about forty powerful men, scattered about the kingdom. They were like giants, standing head and shoulders above everyone else. They were loyal to their king and were trying to get things going for him. However, they all worked independently of each other.

These giants acted as protectors for the people who lived around them. The people felt secure having these strong men to protect them. When the ambassador saw these powerful men, he smiled again, because he noticed how vulnerable they were. They were easy targets, because they were standing alone.

The situation appeared quite hopeless, but something else was happening in the kingdom; something which the ambassador had not noticed, because he had looked in the wrong places. In isolated and insignificant parts of the kingdom, men and women who understood the times had quietly prepared for battle. They had formed into commando units that were trained and ready for warfare. Each member had a task and was equipped to do it. They had learnt to move in unity, because they knew and trusted each other.

The commando units were flexible, so that if one member fell, another could step into his place. By sharing their meagre wealth, they had been able to devote considerable resources to preparation for battle. These men and women were ordinary citizens during the day, but they were now committed, trained, equipped for battle.

In many places throughout the kingdom, similar groups had formed. They were unknown and insignificant people, but they gained strength from their dedication to the king and commitment to each other. Most people did not know they existed, but they were the key to their king's victory. The ambassador had not noticed them, but these commando units would be the stumbling block on which his king would fall. They were unnoticed, but they were at the cutting edge of their kings' work.

The Sequel — The ambassador returned to his kingdom and spoke to his king. He reported that the neighbouring kingdom was very vulnerable. Now was the perfect time to attack the good king. Previously, the evil king had only made minor skirmishes into the other kingdom, mostly under the cover of darkness. He now decided on a full frontal attack.

The evil king amassed his entire army, and marched down the road towards the good king's palace. Before the army got to the border, the king initiated his secret weapon to deal with the forty great men. Many weeks earlier, he had infiltrated skilled bowmen into the other kingdom, instructing each one to track one of the powerful men.

When the bad King gave the signal, the archers attacked the unsuspecting strongmen. In a moment, all of the powerful men were dead or wounded, brought down by a shower of arrows. When the people realised that their protectors had been blown away, they were filled with dread and began to tremble.

When the enemy army arrived at the border post, the border guards were asleep. They were woken by the sound of the large army marching by. When they saw the size of the army, they panicked and ran away. As the great evil army marched into the kingdom, people everywhere were paralysed with fear. The soldiers of the army were wicked ruthless men, who destroyed everything they touched. They cut such a swathe of destruction across the kingdom that it was frightening to watch. The people were so confused they didn't know whether to run away or to surrender and welcome the enemy.

Suddenly there was a stirring. All over the kingdom soldiers came out of their homes and work places. They joined together into commando units, fully equipped, trained and ready for action. One commando team moved to a large bridge over a river that flowed between the enemy army and the king's palace. They set explosives and blew it to pieces. When the enemy army arrived at the river, there was no way to cross.

Another commando unit moved quickly to form an ambush in a narrow gorge that the enemy army had just passed through. Their way of retreat was cut off. Other units attacked the enemy army at points where it was vulnerable. They would move in to inflict damage and then withdraw swiftly to safety. Other commandos set up their artillery batteries on the hills nearby and began to lob shells among the trapped soldiers. Soon panic began to spread through the evil army.

Some of the commando units moved towards the king's palace and took up defensive positions. One team went into the palace. The palace guards were still squabbling among themselves. In the palace, the courtiers were still singing the praises of the king. "Your kingdom extends as far as the eye can see". They seemed oblivious to the threat to their kingdom or the danger to the king.

The members of the commando unit warned the king of the danger. When the courtiers heard what was happening they began to tremble with fear. The palace guards looked like they wanted to run away. The king recognised that the commando unit understood what was happening and were ready for action. He gave them authority over the palace guard. They quickly reorganised the soldiers, establishing order and authority.

Other commandos went into the towns and villages. They gathered the people and taught them the decrees of their king. Many of the people did not even know that they had a king. The commandos organised them into groups and established order in the land. The people were united for the first time and began to harvest the crops together.

A number of the commandos immediately moved over the border into the evil king's kingdom. He was so confident that he had left few soldiers behind to defend his kingdom. These commando units were able to take control of all the strategic positions. Two of the commando units went straight to the bad king's castle. Within a few hours, they had captured the remaining guards and raised the good king's flag over the castle tower.

Back in the other kingdom, the army was trapped on the road. It couldn't move forward and it couldn't move back. The evil king sent out numerous patrols to find a way out, but each one was captured and never returned. Eventually the whole army was in panic and began to run away. The commando units had a tremendous advantage, because they knew the lay of the land like the back of their hands. Many enemy soldiers were killed or captured and only a few escaped back to their own land.

The evil king managed to escape with a few of his soldiers. He got back to his own land, but he couldn't get back to his castle. He fled into the mountains at the very back of his kingdom, where he hid there for many years. He would occasionally go out and make an attack, but he was almost totally powerless.

The good king was able to recover all the territory that he had lost. He was able to extend his authority over most of the enemy king's territory. He was also able to establish order in his own kingdom.

The commandos were unknown and insignificant people. Yet they were to become the key players in a great victory for their King. This victory meant that their King and his Kingdom went unmatched for many, many years.

CHAPTER THIRTEEN

Challenge

Attaining to the whole measure of the fullness of Christ

A large number of Christians are discontented with the modern Church. Many are wandering from church to church looking for something better, but only finding more of the same. Others are so frustrated and disillusioned that they have given up altogether.

These people are not troublemakers or backsliders. They are some of God's best people, but they need a radically different vision to stir their hearts. David built his army from the "discontents and distressed" who gathered around him at Adullam (1 Sam 22: 1,2). These modern "discontents" will be the "mighty men" who do glorious things for God in the days ahead.

He is calling many of them to do something new for him. They should get together with like-minded people and start building according to the pattern outlined in this book.

Twelve Easy Steps
1. Choose three or four people (or couples) to be the elders.
   They should be mature enough to be elders of a small church.
   They should have had experience working together.
   Their ministries should complement each other.
   One should be prophetic and one should be an evangelist.
   Several should have shepherding gifts.
   Balanced ministries are essential.

Friendship is not enough, because friends often have similar ministries.
2. Build foundational relationships.
   Pray together.
   Encourage each other in ministry.
   Agree to accept correction from each other.
   Solve issues honestly.
   Start sharing possessions.
   Support should be spiritual, emotional and material.
3. Seek God's will about a target neighbourhood.
   Seek the person of peace or influence in that neighbourhood.
   This could be a person who has just become a Christian.
   The group should meet in this person's home.
4. Some members of the group should move into the target neighbourhood.
   This will be challenging, but is important for strong fellowship.
5. Start meeting together regularly for worship and fellowship.
   Meetings would be once or twice a week.
   Any day is fine.
   Learn to be led by the Holy Spirit.
6. Focus on the One Another Stuff.
   Work on building relationships.
   Be different from the world.
7. Minister to the people of the neighbourhood.
   Bless someone in financial difficulties.
   Find someone who is sick, and pray for their healing.
   Find the key that will crack open the neighbourhood.
8. Let the Holy Spirit go to work.
   Wait and see what he will do.
   If he does nothing, get on a different bus.
9. Disciple the people who join the Church.
   Build the members into a caring, sharing community.
10. Send some of the elders out to start a new Church.
   Some of the members should soon be ready to be elders.
They should be appointed as elders in place of the original ones.
The original elders can then be sent out to start a new Church.

Suggested Guidelines

The founding members of the new Church should agree on the simple guidelines to set the direction of the Church.

1. Avoid publicity, so the Church can remain in obscurity as long as possible.

   The only ones who need to know are those in the neighbourhood.

   Excessive attention will cause distractions.

   Only the "hard core" should be encouraged to join.

2. Be hard to join and easy to leave.

   The only restraint on the Church should be the bond of love.

   Sharing should be voluntary.

   People should be free to decide their level of commitment.

   People should be free to leave at any time.

3. Only new Christians should be allowed to join the Church.

   Focus on growth through evangelism.

   Avoid drawing frustrated Christians from other churches.

   Work hard to maintain relationships with other churches.

   Avoid conflict with pastors of existing churches.

   Prepare to bless them when hard times come.

4. Christians should only be allowed to join if they live within walking distance of the meeting place.

   There will be Christians from all over the city that want to join.

   Many will say that the Holy Spirit has been speaking to them about this for years.

   Most will be unwilling to make the sacrifice of moving to the new location.

   Understand that they will be a distraction if they are allowed to join.

   Offer to help them start something themselves.

5. Christians should only be allowed to join, if they need to be discipled into the ministry of one of the elders.

   This would be limited to one (or at most two) per elder.

   Each of the elders should be replicating their ministry in another person.

6. Everyone must submit to the elders. That involves:
   Accepting their correction.
   Accepting their guidance.
   Being willing to learn.
7. Do not try to organise a celebration.
   Members can go elsewhere for celebrations.
8. Aim to be radical:
   Focussed on action, not entertainment;
   Choosing simplicity, not materialism;
   Committed to sharing, not individualistic;
   Opposed to the world, but loving the lost;
   Zealous for the Kingdom of God.

Simple but Challenging — The strategy described in this book is fairly simple. It does not require high-powered ministries or brilliant leaders. Starting a Church just needs three people who have:
- the right vision
- the right mix of gifts
- the right commitment
- in the right place

The gifts are easy. One person must be able to share the gospel, one must have a prophetic inclination and one must have the ability to disciple new Christians. They must all have a pure spirit. If any are bitter or hurt, the foundation of the new Church will be flawed.

The right commitment will be tougher. These very different people must have a commitment to working in peace and unity, putting their calling ahead of personal differences. Sharing possessions will not come easy, but is easier than being martyred or crucified.

Getting to the right place may also be a challenge. We will need to get to where the Holy Spirit is moving, but that is where we all want to be.

About the author

Ron McKenzie is a Christian writer
living in Christchurch, New Zealand.
During the 1980s, he served as
the pastor of a church,
but found that he did not fit the role.
He is now employed as an economist
and writes in his spare time.
He is married with three adult children.

Being Church
Where We Live

KINGWATCH BOOKS